Studies in 20th Century

Series edit

The

USSR

Tony Downey

Oxford University Press 1989

Acknowledgements

The publishers would like to thank the following for permission to reproduce photographs:

British Library p. 36; Gunn Brinson p. 43; Camera Press p. 58, p. 64 (and cover); Centre for the Study of Cartoons and Caricatures, Canterbury/© Evening Standard p. 42 (left); Fotomas Index p. 6 (and cover), p. 22 (right); Hulton Deutsch Collection p. 56 (and cover), p. 57 (left); Hulton Picture Company p. 4, p. 15, p. 16, p. 27; © Mail Newspapers p.l.c. p. 51; Mansell Collection p. 8, 9; National Film Archive, London p. 37; Novosti Press Agency p. 5, p. 7, p. 10, p. 17, p. 20, p. 21, p. 24 (right), p. 25 (right), p. 28, p. 34, p. 45, p. 47 (and cover); Popperfoto p. 12, p. 13, p. 14, p. 54, p. 55 (left), p. 57 (right), p. 59; Punch p. 53; Rex Features p. 60 (photo Shone), p. 61 (photo Mikhailov), p. 62; Society for Cultural Relations with the USSR p. 11, p. 35, p. 46; Frank Spooner Pictures p. 63; Topham Picture Library p. 55 (right); Photos by Eileen Tweedy p. 22 (left), p. 23, p. 24 (left), p. 25 (left and cover), p. 26, p. 42 (right).

Oxford University Press, Walton Street, Oxford OX2 6DP

Oxford New York Toronto
Delhi Bombay Calcutta Madras Karachi
Petaling Jaya Singapore Hong Kong Tokyo
Nairobi Dar es Salaam Cape Town
Melbourne Auckland

and associated companies in
Berlin Ibadan

Oxford is the trade mark of Oxford University Press.

© Oxford University Press 1989

ISBN 0 19 913336 0

Typeset by MS Filmsetting Limited
Printed in Hong Kong

Introduction

This series is designed to confront the principal objectives of GCSE history and to provide practical schemes of work which include sources of historical evidence, questions, and mark schemes.

Several assumptions underpin the series. Firstly, evidence is seen to be at the heart of historical study. The evidence in this book comes from a wide range of sources. Each chapter is a unique combination of sources selected to encapsulate, as far as possible, an aspect of the work of the historian. Whereas this book cannot claim to enable students to pursue an exhaustive study of available evidence, the evidence has been selected to provide breadth and balance within the scope of each exercise.

Secondly, the evidence has been selected with a particular historical skill in mind. It will be seen that each chapter is double-headed. The whole book covers fifteen major topics of USSR history, but at the same time uses the individual material of each of these chapters to pursue a particular historical objective. At the end of each chapter can be found questions which meet the coursework requirements of GCSE examining boards.

Content has often been undervalued in the recent historical debate. This series shows how skills and content can complement each other to produce effective and highly motivated learning in history.

Contents

Chapter 1

1905

A study in the causes of discontent

1905 saw the first major disturbance in Russia in the twentieth century. It was a year of strikes and demonstrations, and violence in both the cities and the countryside. This chapter looks at some of the causes of this discontent.

A *Tsar Nicholas II and his family, taken in about 1905.*

B From *Endurance and Endeavour: Russian History 1812–1971*, by J. N. Westwood, 1973.

Historians seeking something good to say about Nicholas sometimes point out that he was a good husband. This he was, but family happiness has never yet saved a dynasty. The lives of Nicholas and Alexandra were tragic because they both had endearing qualities and both found themselves playing roles for which they were quite unfitted. Nicholas had little choice but to rule.

C Extracts from Polovstev's diary, 22 September 1901. Polovstev was a member of the state council that advised the Tsar.

Because of the unrestrained abuse of power by officialdom ... regulations bordering on the ridiculous, the absence of any sound policy discussed in advance, thoughtless interference in affairs, especially appointments by the Empress, the Grand Dukes and Duchesses and the crowds of scoundrels surrounding them, the Russian people are sinking deeper and deeper into misery and oppression.

D Stalin writing in 1901.

Wages are being reduced and bonuses are being taken away. Hours of work are being extended. Workers who make trouble are being blacklisted. The system of fines and beating up is in full swing.

E *Workers living quarters in Putilov, about 1900*

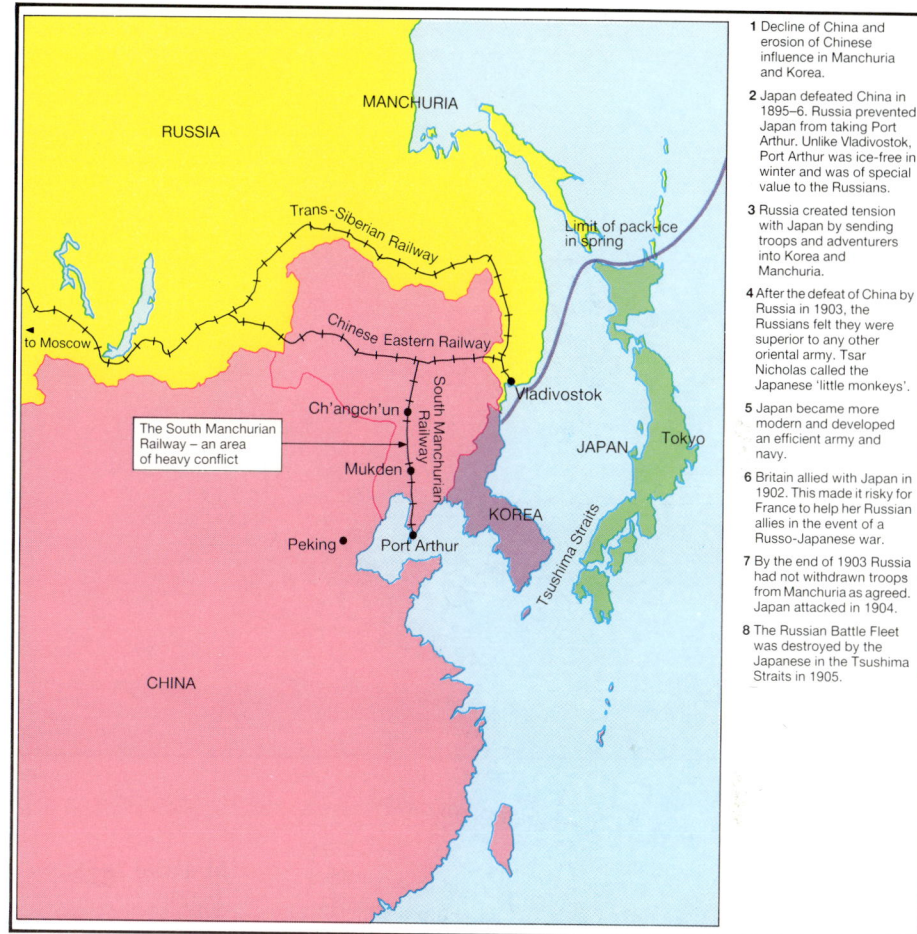

Map labels: RUSSIA, MANCHURIA, Trans-Siberian Railway, Limit of pack-ice in spring, to Moscow, Chinese Eastern Railway, Ch'angch'un, South Manchurian Railway, Vladivostok, The South Manchurian Railway – an area of heavy conflict, Mukden, JAPAN, Tokyo, Peking, Port Arthur, KOREA, Tsushima Straits, CHINA

1 Decline of China and erosion of Chinese influence in Manchuria and Korea.

2 Japan defeated China in 1895–6. Russia prevented Japan from taking Port Arthur. Unlike Vladivostok, Port Arthur was ice-free in winter and was of special value to the Russians.

3 Russia created tension with Japan by sending troops and adventurers into Korea and Manchuria.

4 After the defeat of China by Russia in 1903, the Russians felt they were superior to any other oriental army. Tsar Nicholas called the Japanese 'little monkeys'.

5 Japan became more modern and developed an efficient army and navy.

6 Britain allied with Japan in 1902. This made it risky for France to help her Russian allies in the event of a Russo-Japanese war.

7 By the end of 1903 Russia had not withdrawn troops from Manchuria as agreed. Japan attacked in 1904.

8 The Russian Battle Fleet was destroyed by the Japanese in the Tsushima Straits in 1905.

F From a contemporary Secret Police review of public opinion.

Everyone was carefully watching the new anti-government group: the Social Revolutionaries. But people also kept an eye on the tough measures used by the government against them.

G Plehve, the Minister of the Interior, advised the Tsar:

You do not know the internal condition of Russia. In order to hold back the revolution we need a small victorious war.

I A Russian sailor remembered in 1907:

These noblemen's sons, well cared for and fragile, were capable only of decking themselves out in tunics and epaulettes. They would then stick their snouts in the air, like a mangy horse being harnessed, and bravely scrape their heels on polished floors or dance gracefully at balls or get drunk; in these ways demoralising their subordinates. They didn't even know our names. Corporal punishment was forbidden on paper only, for decency's sake. The sailors were beaten for all kinds of reasons and often. It was considered the natural order of things. There was no way of complaining. We were compelled to eat rotten biscuits and stinking, decaying meat while our officers fatted themselves with the best foods and drank the most expensive wines.

J A contemporary illustration of the Russo-Japanese War

6

K Dr Dillon, *The Daily Telegraph* correspondent in Russia, wrote on 15 July 1904:

Two men on bicycles glided past followed by a closed carriage, which I recognised as that of the all powerful minister [Plehve]. Suddenly the ground below me quivered, a tremendous sound, as of thunder, deafened me. The windows of the houses on both sides of the broad street rattled and the glass of the panes was hurled onto the stone pavements. A dead horse, a pool of blood, fragments of a carriage and a hole in the ground were all parts of my rapid impression. My driver was on his knees devoutly praying and saying that the end of the world had come. Plehve's end was received with semi-public rejoicing. I met nobody who regretted his assassination or condemned the assassins.

L From a Socialist Workers Party pamphlet called *1905: The Great Dress Rehearsal*.

In 1904 when war broke out between Russia and Japan strikes fell to the lowest level for ten years. But after a few months it became clear that the war was a series of blunders and defeats. Patriotic enthusiasm gave way to vexation. Feeling against the war began to connect with the steadily worsening conditions of workers – for the wages of even the best paid were falling by around 25%. These workers turned for organisation and leadership, not to reformers or revolutionaries, but to a young priest, Father Gapon, whose safe legal assembly of St. Petersburg workers had police backing. Yet as Gapon's organisation grew, workers expected more and more action from him. At the beginning of December 1904 the assembly supported its first strikes. Alarmed, the employers victimised four of Gapon's followers. This provoked a stoppage that swiftly spread across the city. It was Gapon's idea to appeal to the Tsar.

M From *The Story of My Life* by Father Gapon, 1905.

St. Petersburg seethed with excitement. All the factories, mills and workshops gradually stopped working, till at last not one chimney remained smoking in that great industrial district ... thousands of men and women gathered incessantly ...

Questions

1 Study Sources **A**, **F** and **I**. What were the causes of discontent in Russia in the years approaching 1905?   10

2 Study Sources **G**, **H**, **J** and **L**
  a) What, according to these sources caused the Russo-Japanese War?   5
  b) What were the consequences of the war for Russia?   5

3 Do you agree that the forms of discontent shown in Sources **K**, **L** and **M** threatened to overthrow the Tsar? Explain your answer carefully with reference to the sources.   10

Chapter 2 Bloody Sunday

*A study in the interpretation and
evaluation of evidence*

The spark that started the revolt of 1905 was the
deaths of many people who were making an appeal to
the Tsar for his help.

A From *Russia in Revolution* by L. Kochan, 1970.

The initial spark was the dismissal of the four
Putilov workmen at the end of December. They
were all members of the assembly [union]. As a
mode of pressure Gapon organised a strike. This
enjoyed instant success. By January 3rd all the
13,000 workers were on strike. Within a few days
... it was virtually a general strike in the Russian
capital. By the 5th, 26,000 had ceased work; by the
7th, 105,000, by the 8th more than 110,000 ...
    The authorities were also not idle. By the 7th
and 8th January they had assembled troops,
including many picked guards regiments, at
electrical gas works, telephone exchanges ... special
concentrations guarded the surroundings of the
Winter Palace. The troops set up braziers to warm
themselves. It needs little imagination to see in St.
Petersburg, in those January days, a city on the
verge of open conflict.

B A contemporary observer talking about Father
Gapon:

For each of his words people were ready to give
their lives; his priest's cassock and crucifix were the
magnet that drew these hundreds of thousands of
tormented people.

C *Father Gapon, c. 1905*

D Letter from Father Gapon to the Tsar, 8 January 1905.

Do not believe the ministers, they are cheating thee in regard to the real state of affairs. The people believe in thee. They have made up their minds to gather at the Winter Palace tomorrow at 2 p.m. to lay their needs before thee ... do not fear anything. Stand tomorrow before the people and accept our humblest petition. I, the representative of the working men and my comrades guarantee the safety of thy person.

E Extracts from the diary of Tsar Nicholas II, 8 January 1905.

A clear, frosty day; there was much activity and many reports. Fredericks came to lunch. Went for a long walk. Since yesterday all the factories and workshops in St. Petersburg have been on strike. Troops have been brought in to strengthen the garrison. The workers have conducted themselves calmly hitherto. At the head of the workers union is some socialist priest: Gapon.

F Extracts from the petition that was brought to the Tsar:

We ask but little ... reduction of the working day to eight hours, the fixing of wage rates in consultation with us. The construction of factories in which it is possible to work without the risk of death from wind, rain and snow. Neither we nor the rest of the Russian people enjoy a single human right. We have been enslaved with the help and co-operation of your officials. Anyone who dares to speak up is jailed or exiled. Government by bureaucracy has brought the country to complete ruin, involved in a shameful war and is leading the country further towards disaster. Popular representation is essential.

G *Gapon's petitioners*

H *Cossaks charge the petitioners*

I From *The Growth of Modern Russia* by John Kennett, 1980.

One hundred and thirty five thousand people had signed the petition, which Gapon had hoped to hand to the Tsar in person. Nicholas, however, had moved his family out of the palace and they were at that moment at Tsarskoe Selo, fifteen miles away ...

The petitioners set out. The people sang hymns and carried portraits of the Tsar. As the crowd filed into the square before the palace the police called upon them to stop and go home. The crowd came on; a trigger happy officer lost his head and gave the order to fire. The sound of hymns gave way to the crack of bullets. Salvo after salvo was poured into the marchers as they broke for cover. Several thousand were wounded and almost one thousand dead were left lying in the snow.

J An eye witness account.

It was an amazing sight. Along came row after row of elderly and solemn workers dressed in their best clothes. Gapon was marching in front carrying a cross and a number of workers were holding icons and portraits of the Tsar. Everyone felt a great sense of excitement. We heard the sound of bugles. The marchers came to a halt, uncertain of what the bugles meant. Just then the cavalry rode out and the first volley of shots rang out. The first volley fired in the air, but the second was aimed at the crowd and a number of people fell to the ground. The crowds began running in every direction. They were now being fired on from behind and we took to our heels. The authorities had made a terrible mistake. The workers believed the Tsar would come out to meet them or at least appear on the balcony but all they got was bullets.

K From *The Story of My Life* by Gapon, 1905.
I saw the swords lifted and falling, the men and women and children dropping to the earth like logs of wood while moans, curses and shouts filled the air.

M From *Russia in Revolution* by L. Kochan, 1970.

For the most part the crowds offered no resistance. But here and there revolutionaries amongst them set up barricades, flourished a red flag or two, broke into the occasional arms store and set telegraph poles on fire.

L *Soldiers aiming at the petitioners*

N Historians have differed greatly in their accounts of the casualties. For example:

Nevsky, *Red Chronicle*, 1922:

> The number of casualties was about one thousand.

Bonch-Bruyevitch (a Bolshevik), 1908:

> The number of casualties was not less than four thousand.

Pete Glatter, Socialist Workers Party Pamphlet, 1985:

> ... troops shot down thousands of unarmed strikers and their families.

John Kennet, *The Growth of Modern Russia*, 1980:

> Several thousand were wounded and almost one thousand dead were left lying in the snow.

Official government figures were: 96 dead and 333 wounded.

O *Soldiers, Soldiers, heroes every one*

Questions

1. What indications are there in sources **A**, **D**, **E**, **G** that the situation in Russia had reached a state of crisis? **6**
2. What do sources **B**, **D**, **F**, **I** and **J** suggest was Gapon's role in the events of Bloody Sunday? **6**
3. a) Use sources **A**, **H**, **I**, **J**, **L** and **M** to trace the stages of the soldiers' actions. **3**
   b) Do the sources help you to understand what caused the soldiers to act in this way? **3**
4. Which of the visual sources provide a reliable picture of what happened? Explain your answer carefully. **6**
5. How do you explain that the estimates of casualties in Source **N** vary so much? **6**

Chapter 3

**The causes of the revolution
of February 1917**

*An exercise in the interpretation of
evidence*

Nineteen-hundred and seventeen was the most dramatic year in Russia in the
twentieth century. There were two revolutions in Russia in this year. The first, in
February, overthrew the Tsar, the second, in October, brought the communists to
power.

A *Russian troops marching to the Central Railway Station at Petrograd, on their way to the war*

B From Muriel Buchanan (daughter of the British
Ambassador To Russia), writing in 1914, when
Germany declared war on Russia.

The processions in the streets carrying the Tsar's
portrait, framed in the flag of the allies, the bands
everywhere playing the National Anthem.
    ... the long unending line of khaki-clad figures
who marched away singing and cheering, tall
bronzed men with honest, open faces with childlike
eyes and a trusting faith in the little father
[Nicholas II], and a sure and certain hope that the
saints would protect them and bring them back to
their villages ...
    Those first days of war! How full we were of
enthusiasm, of the conviction that we were fighting
in a just and holy cause, for the freedom and
betterment of the world! Swept away by the general
air of excitement, we dreamt dreams of triumph
and victory! The Russian steamroller! The British
Navy! The French Guns! The war would be over by
Christmas, the Cossaks would ride into Berlin.

C *Soldiers kneeling before the Tsar, as he blesses them*

D From the memoirs of Rodzianko, President of the Duma (Parliament), writing about the war situation in the winter of 1915.

General Rudski had complained to me of the lack of ammunition and the poor equipment for the men. There was a lack of ammunition and great shortage of boots. In the Carpathians the soldiers fought barefooted. The Grand Duke [Commander in Chief] stated that he was obliged to stop fighting temporarily for lack of ammunition and boots.

E The Tsarina wrote in 1915 to the Tsar advising him to replace Grand Duke Nicholas as Commander in Chief:

I am haunted by our friend's [Rasputin] wish, and know it will be fatal for us and the country if it is not fulfilled.

I have absolutely no faith in Grand Duke Nicholas. You know Nicholas' hatred of Gregory is intense. Russia will not be blessed if her sovereign lets a man of God be persecuted.

F A platoon of Cossaks on the way to the front line

G Rodzianko (leader of the Duma) warned the Tsar in 1915:

If you, sire, should take over the direct leadership of our glorious army, you sire, the last refuge of your people – who will then execute judgement in the case of failure or defeat? It is not clear, sire, that you will then voluntarily have surrendered your inviolable person to the judgement of the people and that is fatal to Russia.

I Letter from Tsarina to Tsar, 28 November 1915.

I must give you over a message from our friend Rasputin prompted by what he saw in the night. He begs you to order an advance near Riga ... otherwise the Germans will settle down through all the winter ... he says we can and we must and I was to write it to you at once.

J The Tsar replies to another request of the Tsarina; this time to changes in the government, that is to appoint Protopopov to be in charge of food supplies.

Thank you for your long letter in which you pass on our friend's (Rasputin's) instructions. It seems to me that this Protopopov is a good man but he has much to do with factories. I must consider this question as it has taken me completely by surprise. Our friend's opinions of people are very strange as you yourself know – therefore one must be very careful, especially to appointments in high office. ... All the changes make my head spin. In my opinion they are too frequent. In any case they are not good for the internal situation of the country as each new man brings with him alterations to the administration.

H *Russian deserters, including officers*

DIE RUSSISCHE ARMEE LÖST SICH VÖLLIG AUF ...

K *Contemporary cartoon of Rasputin*

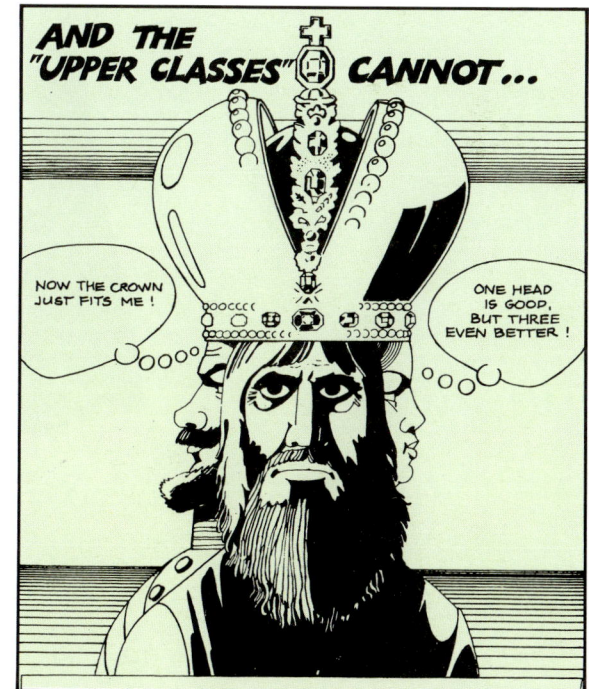

AND THE "UPPER CLASSES" CANNOT...

NOW THE CROWN JUST FITS ME!

ONE HEAD IS GOOD, BUT THREE EVEN BETTER!

L From _Lost Splendour_, Prince Yusopov, 1953.

I aimed at his heart and pulled the trigger. . . . Rasputin lay on his back. Our hearts were full of hope for we were convinced that what had just taken place would save Russia and the Dynasty from ruin and dishonour.

. . . Then a terrible thing happened: with a sudden violent effort Rasputin leapt to his feet foaming at the mouth.

. . . Two shots echoed through the night . . . I saw Rasputin totter and fall beside a heap of snow.

M _Rasputin surrounded by admirers, mostly women_

N

General Krimov:	'The feeling in the army is such that the army will greet with joy the news of a Coup d'Etat.'
Deputy Shingarev:	'The general is right – a Coup d'Etat is necessary, but who will dare undertake it?'
Deputy Shidlevsky:	'We cannot waste pity on the Tsar if he ruins Russia.'
General Brusilov:	'If it comes to a choice between the Tsar and Russia I will take Russia.'
Rodzianko, Leader of the Duma	'I am neither able nor willing to arouse the people against the Tsar.'

P From a police report, 23 February.

9.00 a.m. The workers of the Vyborg District went on strike in protest against the shortage of black bread... The strike spread... so industrial enterprises ceased working...

About 1.00 p.m. The workmen walked in crowds into the streets shouting 'Give us bread'.... order was restored only towards 7.00 p.m.

Q Bolshevik eyewitness to the strikes.

... The tips of the bayonets were touching the breasts of the first row of demonstrators. Behind could be heard the singing of revolutionary songs, in front there was confusion. Women with tears in their eyes were crying out to the soldiers 'Comrades, take away your bayonets, join us!' The soldiers were moved. They threw swift glances at their own comrades. The next moment one bayonet is slowly raised, is slowly lifted above the shoulders of the approaching demonstrators. There is thunderous applause. The triumphant crowd greeted their brothers clothed in the grey cloaks of the soldiery. The soldiers mixed freely with the demonstrators.

O *A queue for bread*

R Telegram from Rodzianko to Tsar, 26 February.

The situation is serious. There is anarchy in the capital. The Government is paralysed. It is necessary immediately to entrust a person who enjoys the confidence of the country with the formation of a government.

On the 27 February:

... The situation is growing worse. Measures should be taken immediately as tomorrow will be too late. The last hour has struck when the fate of the country and Dynasty is being decided.

S Conversation between two Duma Deputies:

Shulgin: It has begun; there is an order to dismiss the Duma. The city is in uproar, let us hurry (to the Duma).

Shingarev: Until the last I continued to hope that they would somehow see the light and make concessions. But no, they dismissed the Duma. That was the last opportunity. An agreement with the Duma, no matter what kind, was the last chance to escape revolution.

T Kerensky (the Prime Minister) remembers:

I was awakened by a voice saying 'get up you are wanted at the Duma at once'. Troops were on their way to the Duma; I knew that the revolution had begun. I said that it was our duty to welcome them and to make common cause with them. The decision was made to form a provisional committee with unrestricted powers. We set up a central body to control the troops and the insurgents.

U *Lenin* by David Shub, 1965.

On March 1st the Tsar received a telegram from the Chief of Staff stating bluntly that the war could be continued only if the Tsar abdicated in favour of his son.

Every moment lost would lead to further demands by the revolutionists who now controlled the railroads and supply service for the army. ... Later all the generals agreed with this: 'But how do I know that it is the desire of all Russia?'. 'Your Majesty' replied one 'circumstances prevent us sending out questionnaires on this matter.'

'... I have made up my mind, I am abdicating ...' He made the sign of the cross.

V Nicholas II issued the following statement:

Internal popular disturbances threaten to have disastrous effect on the future conduct of this war. The destiny of Russia, the honour of our heroic army, the welfare of the people and the whole future of our dear fatherland demand that the war should be brought to a victorious end whatever the cost ...

In these decisive days in the life of Russia we thought it our duty of conscience to bind our people more closely together for a swifter victory. In agreement with the Imperial Duma we thought it well to renounce the throne ... and to lay down supreme power. As we do not wish to part from our beloved son, we transmit the succession to our brother. We direct our brother to conduct the affairs of state in full co-operation with the representatives of the people in the legislative bodies, on those principles to be established by them.

Questions

1 Refer to Sources **A**, **B**, **C**, **F**, and **H**. How did the Russian people's attitude to the war change, according to these sources? 6
2 Read Source **G**. Why might Rodzianko have given this advice to the Tsar? Use Sources **A–H** to explain your answer. 3
3 Use Sources **I**, **J**, **K** and **M** to explain Rasputin's influence on the government. 6
4 What do Sources **L** and **N** suggest about the attitude of the ruling class towards the Tsar? 3
5 Refer to Sources **P**, **Q**, **R** and **S**. Explain how the situation shown in **O** worsened. 6
6 Use Sources **R**, **S**, **T**, **U**, and **V** to explain why the Tsar abdicated. 6

Chapter 4 The October Revolution

An exercise in comparison and evaluation of historical evidence

Different historians interpret the past in different ways. These sources look at how some historians differ about the interpretation of the events of October 1917 which brought the Bolsheviks to power.

A From *How the Revolution was won* by Isaak Mints, Soviet Historian Novosti Press Agency – Moscow, 1987.

On the 10 October at the Central Committee Lenin said that an insurrection was necessary. A majority of the Central Committee voted in favour of immediate action. A Revolutionary military committee was set up to direct the action. Two central committee members voted against the resolution, Zinoviev and Kamenev. They committed treason by sending a letter to a Menshevik newspaper in which they stated their disagreement.

Thus forewarned by traitors the provisional government intensified preparations for crushing the awaited uprising. Units still loyal to the government were summoned from the front. It was risky to act in such conditions and the Bolsheviks postponed the uprising.

Lenin insisted that the insurrection be started before the second Congress of Soviets (25 October). In accordance with Lenin's proposal the Central Committee launched the insurrection on 24 October. Red guard detachments occupied government buildings and took up posts at bridges across the Neva.

On the evening of 24 October the Central Committee asked Lenin to come from his secret hiding place to the Smolny Institute HQ of the insurrection. The leader of the party, the inspirer and organiser of the armed uprising stood at the helm of the revolution. Lenin demanded the immediate capture of the Winter Palace and the arrest of the members of the provisional government gathered there.

B From *V. I. Lenin – A Short Biography* by G. D. Obichkin, Progress Publishers, Moscow, 1976.

On 10 October Lenin showed at the Central Committee that the moment was ripe for the seizure of power by the proletariat and the poor peasants. The Central Committee adopted Lenin's historic resolution on the armed uprising. Kamenev and Zinoviev alone acted as cowards and opposed the resolution … the uprising was carried out with true military precision and still in full accord with Lenin's instructions. The fighting units acted with a high degree of organisation, discipline and co-ordination.

In his guidance of the uprising, Lenin's genius as a leader of the masses, a wise and fearless strategist, who clearly saw what direction the revolution would take, was strikingly revealed.

C From *Russia in Revolution* by Harrison E. Salisbury, Moscow Correspondent, *New York Times*, 1978.

For many years, particularly in the Stalin period, the evidence of Lenin's violent controversy with his colleagues over the uprising was concealed in party archives. Even today the facts are not all known. And even after Lenin's victory of October 10th there was another big argument on the 15th. Lenin had the firm support of 15 out of the 25 members present; but an important faction of the party centred around two of the most prominent members, Kamenev and Zinoviev, who felt the uprising would be a disaster.

Kerensky did not bother to order additional troops into the capital. Bolshevik plans for the coup went forward lackadaisically … anger and energy spent, Lenin now seemed to sink into a kind of lethargy. So far as the record goes he did little or nothing from the 20th to the 23rd of October.

D From *Endurance and Endeavour (A History of Russia)* by J. N. Westwood, Birmingham University, 1986.

There are varying accounts of the meeting of 10 October. The official Soviet history claims that the members received Lenin's proposals enthusiastically, only Zinoviev and Kamenev opposing. But it is more likely that most opposed it at first, and that only after hours of wearying argument did Lenin win a small majority.

E This picture is taken from a film about the October Revolution, called 'October'. It was made in 1927 by Eisenstein to celebrate the revolution

F From *Lenin and the Bolsheviks* by Adam Ulam, Harvard University (US), 1965.

Impatient of waiting, Lenin, in the evening of 24 October merged from his hideout and sought his way to Bolshevik HQ. He was still not convinced that the more timid among his followers would not call the thing off. He had to be present to coax and push them into action even though his presence now in the Smolny could influence the course of events but little and proved to be an embarrassment to the managers of the uprising.

Except for the workers of some factories there was no pro-Bolshevik enthusiasm in the population, only apathy.

G From *The First 50 years: Soviet Russia* by Ian Grey Australian Historian, 1967.

At a secret meeting on 10 October Lenin won the support of the majority of the central committee for his resolution that an armed rising is inevitable and the time is perfectly ripe. Nine out of the twenty two members of this committee were absent. Of those present Zinoviev and Kamenev opposed the resolution. They argued that the party should extend its influence by peaceful means.

Many among even the senior members were also worried. Lenin's demand for an immediate revolt seemed foolhardy. The July revolt had been chaotic. The Red Guard consisted of armed but untrained workers. The Petrograd garrison was unruly and unpredictable. Even in organisations in which the Bolshevik influence was strong there was no support for the uprising.

H *Another scene from 'October'*

I From *The Times* 24 October 1987, Norman Stone Professor of History, University of Oxford.

There were so many entrances to the Winter Palace that the Red Guard forced their way in quite easily; and there were no scuffles -no shooting in the corridors and picture galleries.

When they occupied the Winter Palace there were only six fatal casualties. The coup was staged against a background not of mass enthusiasm but mass apathy.

J From 'Timewatch', a History investigation programme, BBC, 1987.

Cameras at that time couldn't shoot in darkness, so there are no contemporary newsreels or photographs of the revolution. In fact there was no mass storming of the Winter Palace, it was much less dramatic and more disorganised. The American journalist John Reed (a communist sympathiser) gave this account by a sailor who took part in the assault on the Winter Palace:

'About 11 O'clock we broke in the doors and filtered up different stairways one by one, or in little bunches. When we got to the top of the stairs the officer cadets took away our guns; still our fellows kept coming up, little by little until we had a majority. Then we turned around and we took away the cadets guns.'

Eisenstein used live ammunition when making the film 'October'. More people were injured and more damage done to the Palace in making the film than during the revolution itself.

Questions

1. a) How do Sources **A** and **B** compare with Sources **C** and **D** in their account of the meeting of the Central Committee of the Communist Party? 5

   b) How do Sources **A–F** differ in their description of Lenin's role in the Revolution? 5

2. As the sources vary so much in their account of events it may appear hard to rely on them.

   a) How useful are the references at the beginning of each source (e.g. J. N. Westwood, Birmingham University, 1986) in helping us to decide how reliable the source is likely to be? 5

   b) Do you think that any of these sources are biased? Explain why the sources you have chosen are biased. 8

3. What are the limitations of **E** and **H** as historical evidence? Use **I** and **J** to help you answer the question. 7

Chapter 5 The Civil War

An exercise in the interpretation and evaluation of posters as political propaganda

When they assumed power in the October Revolution (Chapter 4) the Bolsheviks closed the Assembly (parliament) and made enemies of the other political parties. They then withdrew from the First World War, which annoyed their allies in the entente (the First World War alliance of Britain, France and Russia). The landowners were furious with the decree to give land to the peasants. The takeover of banks and businesses put the middle classes firmly against the Bolsheviks.

All this led to anti-Communist White Armies being formed from inside and outside Russia. The country was at war from 1918 to 1920. Throughout this Civil War the Soviet artists produced a huge number of propaganda posters for their supporters.

A *Capitalism*

B *The Entente powers, Russia's former allies Britain and France, hiding behind the mask of peace.*

D The League of Nations: Britain, The United States and France

E Three White Army generals: Denikin, Kolchak and Yudenich on leashes.

F *Have you volunteered yet?*

G *Shoulder to shoulder in the defence of Petrograd. (A poster produced when Petrograd was threatened by the White Armies.)*

H *Strike the Pole with all your strength and Wrangle too we'll beat at length. (Poland was one of the interventionist powers. Wrangle was a White Army General.)*

Questions

1 Look carefully at posters **A**, **B** and **C**. What are the artists trying to achieve in these posters? How effectively do they achieve their objective? Support your answers with references to the posters **A**, **B** and **C**.   10

2 Look carefully at posters **D** and **E**. What are the artists trying to achieve here? How effectively do they achieve their objectives?   10

3 Look carefully at posters **F**, **G** and **H**. What are the artists trying to achieve? How effective are these posters in achieving the artists objectives?   10

Chapter 6 The struggle for Power: Stalin v Trotsky

An examination of similarity and difference

Lenin was the undisputed leader of the Bolsheviks. When he died in 1924 there was a struggle for power. The two most powerful men in the party were Stalin and Trotsky. This chapter looks at why Stalin, not Trotsky, succeeded Lenin.

A Lenin's last will and testament:

Comrade Stalin, having become General Secretary, has concentrated an enormous power in his hands; and I am not sure that he always knows how to use that power with sufficient caution ... Stalin is too coarse and this fault is insupportable in the office of General Secretary. Therefore I propose to the comrades to find a way to remove Stalin from the position and appoint it to another man who will in all respects differ from Stalin – more patient, more loyal, more polite, more attentive to comrades.
    Trotsky is the most able man in the party. His defect is in an excess of self-confidence. He is attracted too much by the purely administrative aspect of affairs.

B From *Lev Trotsky, The Eternal Rebel* by Ronald Seth, 1967.

Trotsky was recovering from an illness when Lenin died. He telephoned Stalin to ask when the funeral was to be. Stalin said 'On Saturday, you can't get back in time anyway so we advise you to continue with your treatment'. This was a lie, the funeral was not to be until Sunday and Trotsky could have reached Moscow by then.

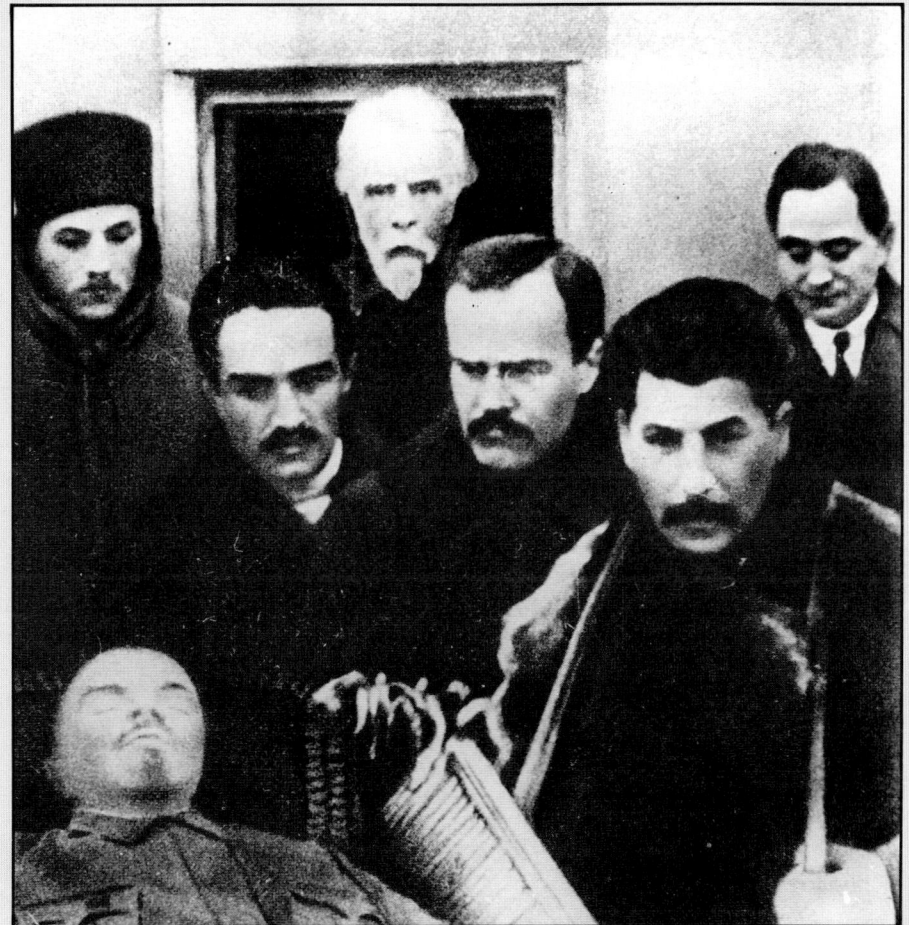

C *Stalin (front right) carrying Lenin's body*

27

D *Mourners at Lenin's funeral*

F From *The Assassination of Trotsky* by Nicholas Mosley, 1972.

How could you have lost power? (Trotsky)
A division began to reveal itself between the leaders ... If I took no part in the amusements ... it was because I hated to inflict such boredom on myself. The new ruling group felt that I didn't fit in; many group conversations would stop the moment I appeared. This was a definite indication that I had begun to lose power.

G From *The Assassination of Trotsky* by Nicholas Mosley, 1972.

Trotsky, during the years of argument, sometimes sat silent- in the party Central Committee, he was once seen reading a novel ...
Trotsky was ill during the winters of '24 and '25 and went on a cure to Berlin in '26. He wrote: 'my high temperature paralyses me at the most critical moments and acted as my opponents most steadfast ally.'...
He and his supporters in congresses and committees were increasingly heckled and shouted down; outside they found their meetings broken up by thugs.

E From *Stalin: Man of Steel* by Elizabeth Roberts, 1968.

There was only one chance for the Communist Party to get rid of Stalin, and that was in May 1924 when Lenin's will was read out to the Central Committee. One eye witness later wrote 'Stalin, sitting on the steps of the rostrum, looked small and miserable; in spite of his self control and show of calm it was clearly evident that his fate was at stake'.
Zinoviev was very anxious not to lose Stalin's help in the struggle against Trotsky and so smoothly and smilingly he suggested that the will be not published, for Comrade Lenin's suspicions of the General Secretary had been proved baseless. The others agreed especially as the will contained criticisms of them too. Lenin's widow jumped to her feet to protest at this suppression of her husbands will, but in vain.
Stalin sat quietly wiping the sweat from his brow.

H From *Animal Farm* by George Orwell, 1974. (*Animal Farm* is regarded by many as an accurate reflection of what happened in post revolutionary Russia. The account of the struggle between Napoleon and Snowball is often used to gain an insight into the differences between Stalin and Trotsky)

Napoleon was a large, rather fierce looking Berkshire Boar, not much of a talker, but with a reputation for getting his own way ...

Snowball was a more vivacious pig than Napoleon, quicker in speech and more inventive but was not considered to have the same depth of character ...

Snowball also busied himself with organising the other animals into what he called animal committees. He was indefatigable in this ...

Napoleon took no interest in Snowball's committees. He said that education of the young was more important than anything that could be done for those who were already grown up ...

Jessie and Bluebell gave birth to nine study puppies. Napoleon took them away from their mothers saying that he would make himself responsible for their education.

Snowball and Napoleon disagreed at every point where disagreement was possible. If one of them suggested sowing a bigger acreage with barley, the other was certain to demand a bigger acreage of oats.·

Each had his own following, and there were some violent debates. At the meetings Snowball often won over the majority by his brilliant speeches, but Napoleon was better at canvassing support for himself in between times. He was especially successful with the sheep. Of late the sheep had taken to bleating and often interrupted the meetings with this. It was noticed that they were especially likely to break into this at crucial moments in Snowball's speeches.

Snowball was full of plans for innovations and improvements. Napoleon produced no plans of his own, but said quietly that Snowball's would come to nothing and seemed to be biding his time.

Until now the animals had been about equally divided in their sympathies (about plans to build a windmill – Snowball for, Napoleon against) but in a moment Snowball's eloquence had carried them away.

Napoleon stood up and casting a peculiar sidelong look at Snowball uttered a high pitched whimper of a kind no one had heard him utter before.

At this there was a terrible baying sound outside, and nine enormous dogs wearing brass studded collars came bounding into the barn. They dashed straight for Snowball who only sprang from his place just in time to escape their snapping jaws. In a moment he was out of the door and they were after him. Too amazed and frightened to speak all the animals crowded through the door to watch the chase. Silent and terrified, the animals crept back into the barn. In a moment the dogs came bounding back. At first no one had been able to imagine where these creatures came from but the problem was soon solved: they were the puppies whom Napoleon had taken away from their mothers and reared privately. Though not yet fully grown they were huge dogs and as fierce looking as wolves.

He announced that from now on the Sunday morning meetings would come to an end. In future all questions relating to the working of the farm would be settled by a special committee of pigs presided over by himself. There would be no more debates.

I From *Stalin: Man of Steel* by Elizabeth Roberts, 1968.

Trotsky's power was in the formidable Red Army of which he was supreme commander. There was little doubt that it would support him if he tried to seize power. Stalin therefore proposed to the Central Committee of the party that Comrade Trotsky should be removed from his position as Head of the Army, for the war had been over for some time and it was a pity to waste his brilliant talents. Comrade Trotsky should be put in charge of the electrification of the USSR.

The Committee duly elected Trotsky to this new post.

J From *Lev Trotsky, The Eternal Rebel* by Ronald Seth, 1967.

In January 1925 he was relieved of his post as Commisar for war without consultation with him and put in charge of electricity. The object was to isolate him from the party by submerging him in routine work.

He made no protest, but plunged into his new work with his old vigour.

K From *Europe, Grandeur and Decline* by A. J. P. Taylor, 1967.

Trotsky never adapted himself to the needs of pratical work in the party. He joined the Bolshevik Party only in the summer of 1917, some two months before he was to carry it to supreme power. The possession of a party card mean nothing to him. His position in the world did not depend on the accuracy of a filing cabinet.

The seizure of power in October was Trotsky's work, and Lenin acknowledged this immediately afterwards with supreme generosity when he proposed that Trotsky be put at the head of the new revolutionary government.

It was Trotsky who created the armies (in the civil war), determined the strategy and inspired the soldiers.

Questions

1 Read source **A**. What does it tell you of Lenin's doubts about Stalin? Despite the criticism by Lenin, why, according to **E**, did Stalin survive? 5

2 We can learn a great deal about Stalin's character by examining how he, not Trotsky, became the ruler of Russia. What do Sources **B**, **C** and **I** reveal of Stalin's character? 7

3 a) What, according to Sources **A**, **I** and **K** were Trotsky's strengths as a potential leader? 4

   b) Despite these strengths, Trotsky asked of himself 'How could you have lost power?' How do Sources **B**, **F**, **G**, **J** and **K** suggest that it was his own fault that he lost power? 6

4 What picture does Orwell give us of Trotsky (Snowball) and Stalin (Napoleon) in *Animal Farm* Source **H**? Do you agree with his interpretation? 8

Chapter 7 The industrialisation of Russia through the Five Year Plans

An exercise in the use of statistics as historical evidence

Stalin claimed that Russia was fifty, even one hundred, years behind the industrialised nations. He wanted to make up that deficit in ten years. To do this he set targets for every section of industry, which were to be achieved in five years. These sources show: a) the situation before the Five Year Plans, b) the targets that were set, c) the actual achievement of these targets.

The statistics in this chapter are adapted from *An economic history of the USSR* by Alec Nove, 1969.

A *Production of selected items, 1913–51*

Product	1913	1921	1928	1933	1940	1945	1953
Agricultural							
Grain (*million tons*)	86	36	73	69	95	75	83
Cows (*millions*)	29	25	29	19	28	23	25
Pigs (*millions*)	23	13	19	10	27	11	29
Industrial							
Electrical power (*billion kWh*)	2	0·5	5	16	48	43	119
Crude oil (*million tons*)	9	4	12	22	31	19	48
Coal (*million tons*)	29	9	35	76	165	149	301
Steel (*million tons*)	4	0·2	4	7	18	12	34
Trucks (*millions*)	0	0	0·7	4	14	7	24
Tractors (*millions*)	0	0	0·1	7	3	0·7	10
Consumer							
Automobiles (*millions*)	0	0	0	1	0·5	0·5	6
Washing machines (*millions*)	0	0	0	0	0	0	0·5
Cameras (*millions*)	0	0	0	3	35	0	46
Radio sets (*millions*)	0	0	0	3	16	1·5	129
Shoes (*million pairs*)	60	28	58	90	211	63	238

B *Rural and urban population, 1920–1939*

Year	Rural population (millions)	Urban population (millions)
1920	110·0	20·8
1923	119·9	21·6
1926	120·7	26·3
1929	126·7	27·6
1931	128·5	33·6
1933	125·4	40·3
1939	114·5	56·1

C *The first Five Year Plan: targets and achievements*

Item	1927 (actual)	1932/3 (plan)	1932/3 (actual)
National Income (*milliard roubles*)	24·4	49·7	45·5
Gross industrial production (*milliard roubles*):	18·3	43·2	43·3
a) Producer's goods	6·0	18·1	23·1
b) Consumer's goods	12·3	25·1	20·2
Gross agricultural production (*in milliard roubles*)	13·1	25·8	16·6
Electricity (*100 million kWh*)	5·05	22·0	13·4
Coal (*million tons*)	35·4	75·0	64·3
Oil (*million tons*)	11·7	22·0	21·4
Pig iron (*million tons*)	3·3	10·0	6·2
Steel (*million tons*)	4·0	10·4	5·9
Total employed labour force (*millions*)	11·3	15·8	22·8

D *A detailed account of the second Five Year Plan*

Item	1923 (actual)	1937 (Plan)	1937 (actual)
National Income (*million roubles*)	45 500	100 000	96 000
Gross industrial production (*million roubles*):	43 000	92 000	95 000
a) Producers goods	23 100	45 000	55 200
b) Consumer's goods	20 200	47 200	40 300
Gross agricultural production (*million roubles*)	13 000	36 000	20 100
Electricity (*milliard kWh*)	13·4	38·0	36·2
Coal (*million tons*)	64·3	152·5	128·0
Oil (*million tons*)	22·3	46·8	28·5
Pig Iron (*million tons*)	6·3	16·0	14·5
Steel (*million tons*)	5·9	17·0	17·7
Employment (*millions*)	22·9	28·9	26·9
Average money wage (*roubles per annum*)	1 427	1 755	3 047
Retail price index (*1933 = 100*)	100	65	180
Volume of retail trade (*1933 = 100*)	100	250·6	150

E *Comparative statistics of Russia with the other great powers, 1913 and 1940*

1) 1913 Country	Pig iron (millions tons)	Steel (million tons)	Coal (million tons)
Russia	4·8	5·2	36·0
USA	30·9	31·3	509·9
UK	10·3	7·7	287·0
Germany	19·3	18·3	190·0
France	5·2	4·7	40·8

2) 1940 Country	Pig iron (million tons)	Steel (million tons)	Coal (million tons)
Russia	14·9	18·4	164·6
USA	31·9	47·2	359·0
UK	6·7	10·3	227·0
Germany	18·3	22·7	186·0
France	6·0	6·1	45·5

Questions

1 Look carefully at sources **A**, **C** and **E**. What according to these sources were the main aims of Soviet economic policy and what were the principal results? 6
2 Use the statistics in source **B**, and in the light of source **A** describe and explain the change in population distribution in the Soviet Union. 6
3 How would you use the evidence in **C** and **D** to judge the effect that the plans had on the standard of living in the Soviet Union? 6
4 Stalin launched his industrialisation programme by saying 'we are fifty or a hundred years behind the advanced nations. We must make good the lag in ten years'. How far does source **E** show 'caught up' by 1940? 6
5 What are the strengths and weaknesses of statistics as historical evidence as revealed by these sources? 6

Chapter 8 Collectivisation of agriculture

An exercise in empathy

The following pages look at how people felt about the huge changes in farming that Stalin insisted upon. Stalin wanted to improve agricultural output by making all the small farms into giant collective farms. To understand the scale on which all this was done, you should remember that most of the Russian people were farmers (peasants). Consider also the huge size of Russia: it occupies one sixth of the land surface of the earth. Many, many millions were affected by this dramatic and fundamental change to their lives.

A Stalin talking to party congress in 1927:

What is the way out? The way out is to turn the small and scattered peasant farms into large united farms based on cultivation of the land in common ... on the basis of a new higher technique. The way out is to unite the small and dwarf peasant farms gradually but surely, not by pressure but by example and persuasion into large farms based on common, co-operative collective cultivation of the land ... There is no other way out.

B Stalin speaking to the peasants in Siberia in 1928:

I have made a tour of your territory and have had the opportunity to see for myself that your people are not seriously concerned to help the country emerge from the grain crisis. You have had a bumper harvest ... Your grain surpluses this year are bigger than ever before. Yet the plan for collecting grain is not being fulfilled. Why? ... Look at the Kulak (rich peasant) farms: their barns and sheds are crammed with grain ... You say the Kulaks are demanding an increase in prices up to three times those fixed by the government. The effect will be that our towns and Red Army will be poorly supplied and threatened with hunger. Obviously we cannot allow that.

C Stalin addressing the party in 1929:

We must break down the resistance of the Kulaks and deprive this class of its existence. We must eliminate the Kulaks as a class. We must smash the Kulaks ... we must strike at the Kulaks so hard as to prevent them rising to their feet again. We must annihilate them as a social class.

D This account shows how a group of peasants reacted when they heard that their land was to be collectivised. It comes from *Virgin Soil* by Mikhail Sholokov, 1977.

Stock was slaughtered every night in Gremyachy Log. Hardly had dusk fallen when the muffled, short bleats of sheep, the death squeals of pigs, or the lowing of calves could be heard. Both those who had joined the Kolkhoz (collective farm) and individual farmers killed their stock. Bulls, sheep, pigs, even cows were slaughtered, as well as cattle for breeding. The horned stock of Gremyachy was halved in two nights. The dogs began to drag entrails about the village. Cellars and barns were filled with meat. The co-operative sold about two hundred poods (about 36 lbs) of salt in two days, that had been lying in stock for eighteen months. 'Kill, its not ours any more . . . Kill, they'll take it for meat anyway . . . Kill, you won't get any meat in the Kolkhoz'. And they killed. They ate until they could eat no more. Young and old suffered from stomach ache. At dinner time tables groaned under boiled and roasted meat. At dinner time everyone had a greasy mouth, everyone hic-coughed as if at a wake. Everyone blinked like an owl, as if drunk from eating.

E *A party worker talking to the peasants about collectivisation*

F From *Red Bread*, 1931, a book by Hindus about Russian reactions to collectivisation.

There was a time when we were neighbours. Now we are either very poor peasants or fairly wealthy peasants or Kulaks. And we are supposed to have a class war. But it is other things that worry us . . . whoever heard of such a thing . . . to give up our land and cows etc., to work all the time and divide everything with others?

We, strangers are supposed to be like one family. Can we dull witted peasants make it go without scratching each others faces? We won't be even sure of having enough to eat. No more potatoes of our own. Everything will be rationed out by orders. We shall be like mere serfs on the landlords estate.

The Communist among them then said 'What hope is there for you if you remain on your individual pieces of land? From year to year as you increase in population you divide and sub-divide you strips of land. Under your present system nothing is ahead of you but ruin and starvation. You accuse us of making false promises. Let us see! Last year you got a school house and now aren't you glad your children can attend school?'

'The Kolkhoz is different' shouted the old man. The Communist replied 'Of course it's different, different but better. Isn't it time you stopped thinking each one for himself? You Kulaks, you will never accept the new order. You love to fatten on other peoples' blood. But we know how to deal with you. We will wipe you off the face of the earth.'

G The Red Army was sent to deal with those peasants who wouldn't join the collective. A Red Army Commander remembers:

I am an old Bolshevik. I worked in the underground against the Tsar and then I fought in the Civil War. Did I do all that in order that I should now surround villages with machine guns and order my men to fire indiscriminately into crowds of peasants? Oh no, no!

H From *Let History Judge* by R. Medvedev, 1971.

Soon mass transportation of Kulaks took place. In unheated railway cars thousands of peasants with their wives and children, went east to the Urals, Kazakhstan and Siberia. Many thousands died en route from hunger, cold and disease. In winter, during a severe frost, a large group of Kulaks were being taken in wagons three hundred kilometres away. One, unable to endure the crying of a baby sucking its mothers empty breast, grabbed the child and dashed its head against a tree.

An American correspondent set at two million the approximate number of those deported and exiled in 1929–30. But the truth appears far worse if we realise that de-Kulakisation continued without let-up through the following years. Official figures vary between five and ten millions.

I *Red Army soldiers working with the peasants*

J Cartoon showing that the peasants cultivated their own private plots at the expense of the collective farm

КРОКОДИЛ

№ 16 ИЮНЬ МОСКВА 1939 · ИЗДАНИЕ ГАЗЕТЫ „ПРАВДА" ГОД ИЗДАНИЯ XVIII · ЦЕНА НОМЕРА 60 КОП.

Рис. А. Каневского

ОБМАН ЗРЕНИЯ
— Ты не смотри, что у Кошкина хата с краю. Это у него колхоз с краю, а хата, наоборот, в центре.

L From a conversation between Churchill and Stalin during the Second World War. Churchill relates:

'Tell me', I asked, 'have the stresses of this war been as bad to you personally as carrying through the policy of the collective farms?'

This subject immediately roused Stalin. 'Oh no', he said, 'the collective farm policy was a terrible struggle'.

'I thought you would have found it bad', said I, 'because you were not dealing with a few score thousands of aristocrats or big land owners, but with millions of small men'.

'Ten millions', he said holding up his hands. 'It was fearful. Four years it lasted. It was absolutely necessary for Russia, if we were to avoid periodic famines, to plough the land with tractors. We must mechanise our agriculture. When we gave tractors to the peasants they were all spoiled in a few months. Only the collective farms with workshops could handle tractors. We took the greatest trouble to explain it to the peasants. It was no use arguing with them. After you have said all you can to a peasant he says he must go home and consult his wife. After he has talked it over he always answers that he does not want the collective farm, and he would rather do without the tractors.'

'These were what you call Kulaks?' I asked.

'Yes', he said, but he did not repeat the word. After a pause he said 'it was all very bad and difficult – but necessary'.

K From *Stalin: Man of Steel* by Elizabeth Roberts, 1968.

The peasants soon discovered and have continued to discover innumerable small ways of 'getting their own back' on the collectives. In one farm, it is reported, the headman (who is a state-appointed official) bought 1000 chickens out of the collective's profits. He gave them to the peasants and promised that they could keep half when the birds were fully grown, although the other half must be returned to the collective. Later when the headman inspected the returned birds, he found that ninety per cent were roosters!

Question

1 Use the sources to show the possible attitudes and feelings of the people involved in the collectivisation of a village.

30

Chapter 9 The Gulag Archipelago

An exercise in the use of literature as historical evidence

The Gulag Archipelago is a huge work of literature. Alexander Solzhenitsyn has written it from his own experiences of imprisonment and forced labour. He also tells the stories of numerous victims of Stalin's terror and of Soviet prisons and labour camps. He wanted to tell the story of a vicious period that killed, ruined and deformed millions of people.

At the beginning of the book he says 'In this book there are no fictitious persons nor fictitious events. People and places are named with their own names. If they are identified by initials instead of names it is for personal considerations. If they are not named at all it is only because human nature (bad memory?) had failed to preserve their names.

But it all took place just as it is here described!'

A scene from the film 'One day in the life of Ivan Denisovitch'.

A From a section of *The Gulag Archipelago* that is concerned with search and arrest by the Secret Police.

... and nothing is sacred in a search. During the arrest of the locomotive engineer, Inoshin, a tiny coffin stood in his room containing the body of his newly dead child. The police dumped the child's body out of the coffin and searched it. They shake sick people out of their sick beds and they unwind bandages to search beneath them ... In 1937 a woman came to the reception room of the Novocherkrassk NKVD (Secret Police) to ask what she should do about the unfed unweaned infant of a neighbour who had been arrested. They took her and tossed her into a cell.

B

Several dozen young people got together for some kind of musical evening which had not been authorized ahead of time by the GPU. They listened to music and then drank tea. They got the money for the tea by voluntarily contributing their own Kopeks! It was quite clear of course that this music was a cover for counter-revolutionary sentiments and that the money was being collected not for tea but to assist the dying world bourgeois. And they were all arrested and given from three to ten years – Anna Shipnikera getting five, while Ivan Nikolayevich, Varentser and the other organisers of the affair who refused to confess were shot.

C

A district party conference was under way in Moscow Province. At the conclusion of the conference a tribute to Comrade Stalin was called for. The small hall echoed with stormy applause rising to an ovation: for three minutes, four minutes, five minutes … The older people were panting from exhaustion. The applause went on six, seven, eight minutes. The NKVD were watching to see who quit first.

The director of the local paper factory aware of all the falsity sat down after eleven minutes. And, oh what a miracle took place where had all the enthusiasm gone? To a man everyone else stopped dead and sat down.

That same night the paper factory director was arrested. His interrogator told him 'Don't ever be the first to stop applauding'.

D

A woman was going home late one night … she passed some people working to free a truck that had gotten stuck. It turned out to be full of corpses – hands and legs stuck out from beneath the canvas. They wrote down her name and the next day she was arrested. The interrogator asked her what she had seen. She told him truthfully. She was sentenced to ten years for anti-Soviet agitation.

E

A further method used to extract a confession was to blackmail your love for your family.

They would threaten to arrest everyone you loved. Sometimes this would be done with sound effects. Your wife has already been arrested but her further fate depends on you. They are questioning her in the next room – just listen! And through the wall you can actually hear a woman weeping and screaming. (After all they all sound alike; you're hearing it through a wall; Sometimes they simply play a recording of the voice of a typical wife).

Or they give you a letter to read and the handwriting is exactly like hers. 'I renounce you! After the filth they have told me about you I don't need you any more.'

(And since such wives do exist in our country and such letters as well you are left to ponder in your heart: Is that the kind of wife she really is?).

F

A newly arrested prisoner was without explanation given a spade and ordered to dig a pit of the exact dimensions of a grave. When the prisoner had dug deeper than his waist they ordered him to stop, and sit down on the bottom. One guard kept watch over several such pits. They kept the accused in this desert with no protection from the Mongolian sun and with no warm clothing against the cold of the night, but no tortures: why waste time on tortures? The ration they gave was three and a half ounces of bread per day and one glass of water. Lieutenant Chulpenyev spent a month imprisoned in this way. Within 10 days he was swarming with lice. After 15 days he was summoned to interrogation for the first time.

G

In 1938 Ivanor Razannik found 140 prisoners in a cell intended for 25 – with toilets so overburdened that prisoners were taken to the toilet only once a day, sometimes at night. And the same was true of their outdoor walk as well. It was Ivanor Razannik who in the Lubyanka reception kennel calculated that for weeks at a time there were three persons for each square yard of floor space (just as an experiment try to fit three people into that space!).

In this kennel there was neither ventilation nor a window, and the prisoners body heat and breathing raised the temperature to 40°C or 45°C. Their naked bodies were pressed against one another and they got eczema from one another's sweat. They sat like that for weeks at a time and were given neither fresh air nor water – except for gruel and tea in the morning.

I

In 1932, at one time 265 prisoners were awaiting execution in Leningrad's Kristy prison alone. (This is the testimony of B who brought food to the cells of the prisoners condemmed to be shot). And during the whole year it would certainly seem that more than 1000 were shot in Kristy alone . . .

It is also believed that a quarter of Leningrad was purged – cleaned out – in 1934–55. Let this be disproved by those who have the exact statistics and are willing to publish them . . . Where is that special archive we might be able to penetrate in order to read the figures? There is none. Therefore we dare only mention these figures mentioned in rumours that were quite fresh in 1939–40, coming from high ranking secret policemen who had been arrested (And they really knew!). They said that during 1937/38 half a million political prisoners had been shot.

H

The prison doctor was the interrogator's and executioner's right hand man. The beaten prisoner would come on to the floor only to hear the doctor's voice: 'you can continue, the pulse is normal'. After a prisoner's 5 days and nights in a punishment cell the doctor inspects the frozen naked body and says: 'you can continue'. If a prisoner is beaten to death he signs the death certificate 'Cirrhosis of the liver', or 'Coronary occlusion'.

He gets an urgent call to a dying prisoner in a cell and he takes his time. And whoever behaves differently is not kept on (as a doctor) in the prison.

Questions

1. What do Sources **A–D** tell you about:
   a) the reasons for arrest?
   b) the methods used to arrest people?   8
2. Use Sources **E**, **F**, **G** and **H** to describe life inside the camps.   9
3. Refer to the *italicised* sections in **B** and **C**. What do they reveal about the attitude of the author?   5
4. How reliable do you think these accounts are as evidence of life during the purges? In your answer consider how the author gathered his information. Use the introduction and Sources **G** and **I** to help you.   8

Chapter 10 Russian Relations with Germany 1938–1944

An exercise in the use of cartoons as historical evidence

The historian can use almost anything from the past as evidence: letters, diaries, government papers, newspapers or cartoons. The cartoonists usually comment on important events and the people (usually politicians) involved in them. The following sources show how cartoonists saw the changing foreign policy of Russia from 1938 to 1943.

A *Baby in the cradle*

B An account of Soviet-German relations 1938–39 (adapted from *A History of the USSR* by Kukushkin – Progress Publishers Moscow 1981).

Britain, France and the USA by rejecting the idea of collective security proposed by the USSR played into the hands of the aggressors (Germany). The great powers (Britain, France and the USA) wanted to direct the German fascist aggression eastwards, against the USSR. The disgraceful Munich deal (where Britain and France allowed Germany to take the Sudetenland from Czechoslovakia) and the Anglo-German and Franco-German Treaties of non-aggression that followed helped Germany to turn her aggression towards the USSR.

The Munich policy of appeasement pushed Europe to the brink of war.

At the same time the Soviet Union tried to make peace. In March 1939 the Soviet Union opened talks with Britain and France to discuss ways of preventing fascist aggression. These talks which lasted until August 1939 showed how unwilling Britain and France were to set up collective security (a united front against Hitler). As a result the Soviet Union stood alone in the face of the growing fascist menace. In this situation the USSR took the only correct decision: when she was asked by Germany to make a treaty of non-aggression the Soviet Union agreed. The Russo-German non-aggression pact was signed in August 1939. The Soviet Union agreed to this pact with Germany only when it became clear that Britain and France were totally unwilling to stand up to the fascist aggressors with the USSR.

Some western historians tried to prove in vain that the pact helped to start the Second World War. The truth is it helped to stop the united front against the USSR and it gave the USSR precious time in which to strengthen its defences. The Soviet government was clearly aware that Germany would at some time attack Russia.

C *Twist the dagger out of that paw*

Чтоб из этой лапы выпал нож —
Антифашистского фронта силы множь!

D *On the Great European Road*

E *Under the broomstick*

F *Rendezvous*

42

H *Pincer movement*

I *Fritzies transformed*

ПРЕВРАЩЕНИЕ „ФРИЦЕВ" ОКНО ТАСС №640

КУКРЫНИКСЫ-42.

ТО НЕ ЗВЕРИ С ДИКИМ ВОЕМ
В БУРНЫЙ РИНУЛИСЬ ПОТОК,
ЭТО ГИТЛЕР СТРОЙ ЗА СТРОЕМ
ГОНИТ „ФРИЦЕВ" НА ВОСТОК.

ЗДЕСЬ, ГДЕ ОКНА ВСЕ – БОЙНИЦЫ,
ЗДЕСЬ, ГДЕ СМЕРТЬ ТАЯТ КУСТЫ,
ЗДЕСЬ, ГЛОТНУВ ЧУЖОЙ ЗЕМЛИЦЫ,
ОДУРАЧЕННЫЕ „ФРИЦЫ"
ПРЕВРАЩАЮТСЯ В КРЕСТЫ.

ГИБЕЛЬ СВОЛОЧИ НЕМЕЦКОЙ
НЕ ЧЬЕ – ЛИБО КОЛДОВСТВО,
ЭТО – АРМИИ СОВЕТСКОЙ
БОЕВОЕ ТОРЖЕСТВО!

ХУДОЖНИКИ-КУКРЫНИКСЫ.   ТЕКСТ-ДЕМЬЯН БЕДНЫЙ.

урал фронту

Questions
1 Refer to the passage by Kukushkin (**B**) and cartoons **A**, **C**, **D** and **E**. In what ways do the cartoons support the views expressed in the passage? 7
2 Cartoon **F** is a British view of the Russo-German pact. Compare the cartoonist's view of the pact with that of Kukushkin. 7
3 Refer to cartoons **G–J** How do each of the cartoonists make their point about the way in which Germany would be defeated? 6
4 Of what value are these cartoons to the student of Russo-German relations from 1936 to 1944? 10

Chapter 11 The Great Patriotic War

An exercise in empathy

When Germany attacked Russia in June 1941, Stalin entreated his fellow countrymen to defend their motherland. He appealed to their love of their country, not their love of communism. The war is consequently known as the Great Patriotic War. The Russian losses were enormous, more than any other country. The people suffered terribly throughout the war.

A From Stalin's broadcast to the nation after the German invasion of Russia, June 1941.

Comrades, citizens, brothers and sisters, fighters of our army and navy. I am speaking to you my friends.

The enemy is cruel. He is out to seize our lands ... our grain and oil. He is out to restore the rule of landlords, to turn our people into the slaves of German Princes. In case of a forced retreat the enemy must not be left a single engine, a single pound of grain or gallon of fuel. All valuable property including grain and fuel that cannot be withdrawn must be destroyed without fail. In areas occupied by the enemy guerillas must be formed, sabotage groups must be organised to combat the enemy ... to blow up bridges and roads.

When he heard this broadcast General Fedyuninsky said 'we suddenly seemed to feel much stronger'.

B From *Hitler: A Study in Tyranny* by Alan Bullock, 1962.

When the German Armies entered the Ukraine and the Baltic States they were looked upon as liberators. The treatment and local population received (from the SS) destroyed these illusions. Ignoring all that could have been done to drive a wedge between the people and the Soviet Government Hitler preferred the peoples of Eastern Europe as .. fit only for slave labour. His Commissioner for the Ukraine said 'the least German worker is racially and biologically a thousand times more valuable than the population here'.

C *Families in the Ukraine returning to their village which has been destroyed by the Germans.*

D Guderian (a German general) recalls his meeting with an old, retired Tsarist general. The Tsarist general said:

> If only you had come twenty years ago, we should have welcomed you with open arms. But now it is too late. We were just beginning to get on our feet, and now you arrive and throw us back twenty years so that we will have to start from the beginning all over again. Now we are fighting for Russia and in that cause we are all united.

E From *War and Social Change in the Twentieth Century* by Arthur Marwick, 1974.

People worked twelve, thirteen, sometimes fourteen or fifteen hours a day; they knew that never was their work more urgently needed than now. Many died in the process. They knew what losses were being suffered by the soldiers, and they – in the distant rear did not grumble much. While the soldiers were suffering and risking so much it was not for the civilians to shirk even the most crippling and heartbreaking work. At the height of the Siberian winter some people had to walk to work – sometimes three, four, six miles and then work for twelve hours or more and then walk back again day after day, month after month.

F From an article by A. Werth, *Sunday Times* journalist, 1964.

A peculiar form of profiteering grew up in Moscow: the owner of a cigarette would charge any willing passers-by two roubles (about 5p) for a puff. There were plenty of buyers.

G The body of one of the 800,000 victims of the Leningrad Blockade being dragged through the streets of the city

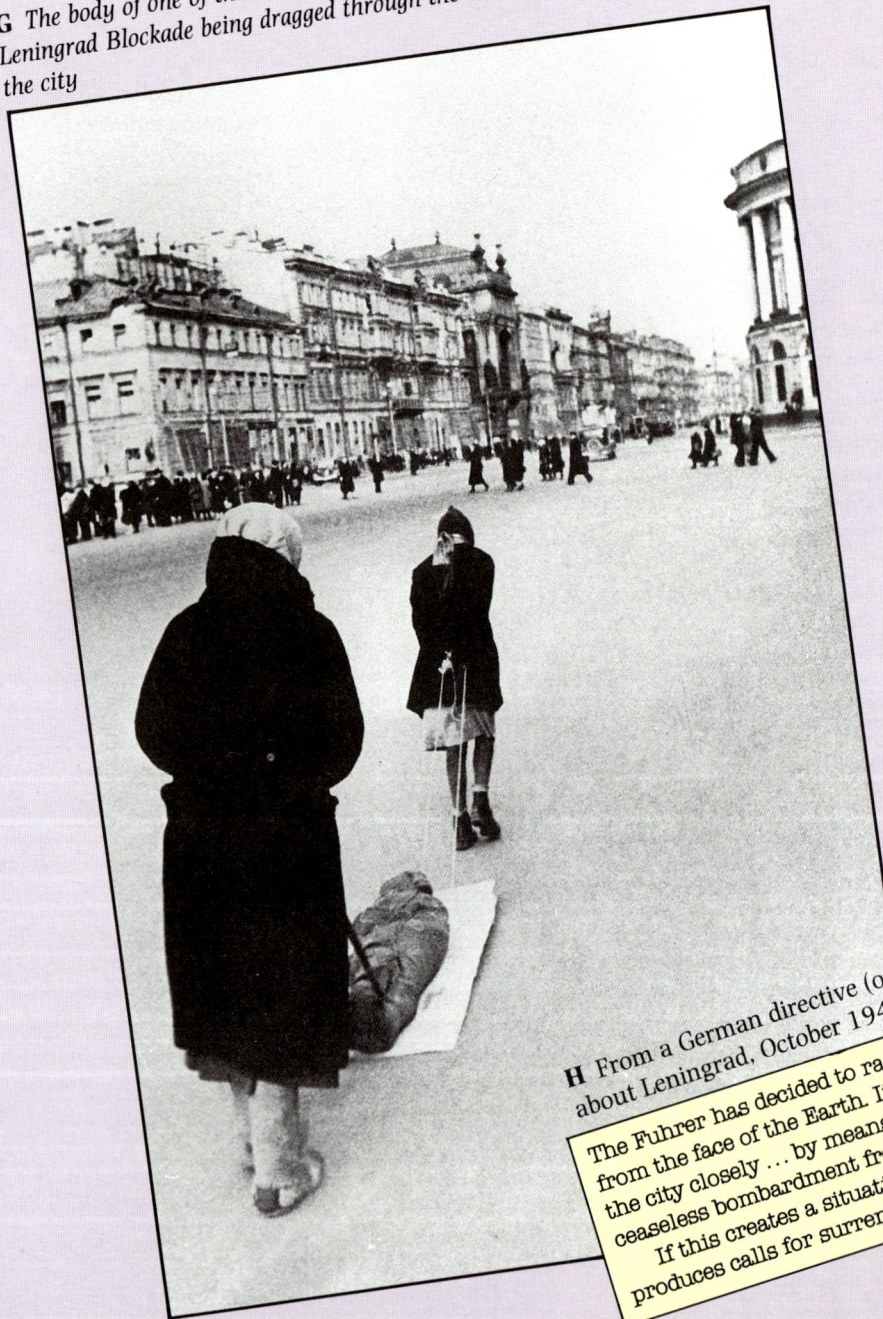

H From a German directive (orders for the Army) about Leningrad, October 1941.

The Führer has decided to raze the city of Leningrad from the face of the Earth. It is proposed to blockade the city closely ... by means of artillery, with ceaseless bombardment from the air.

If this creates a situation in the city which produces calls for surrender they will be refused.

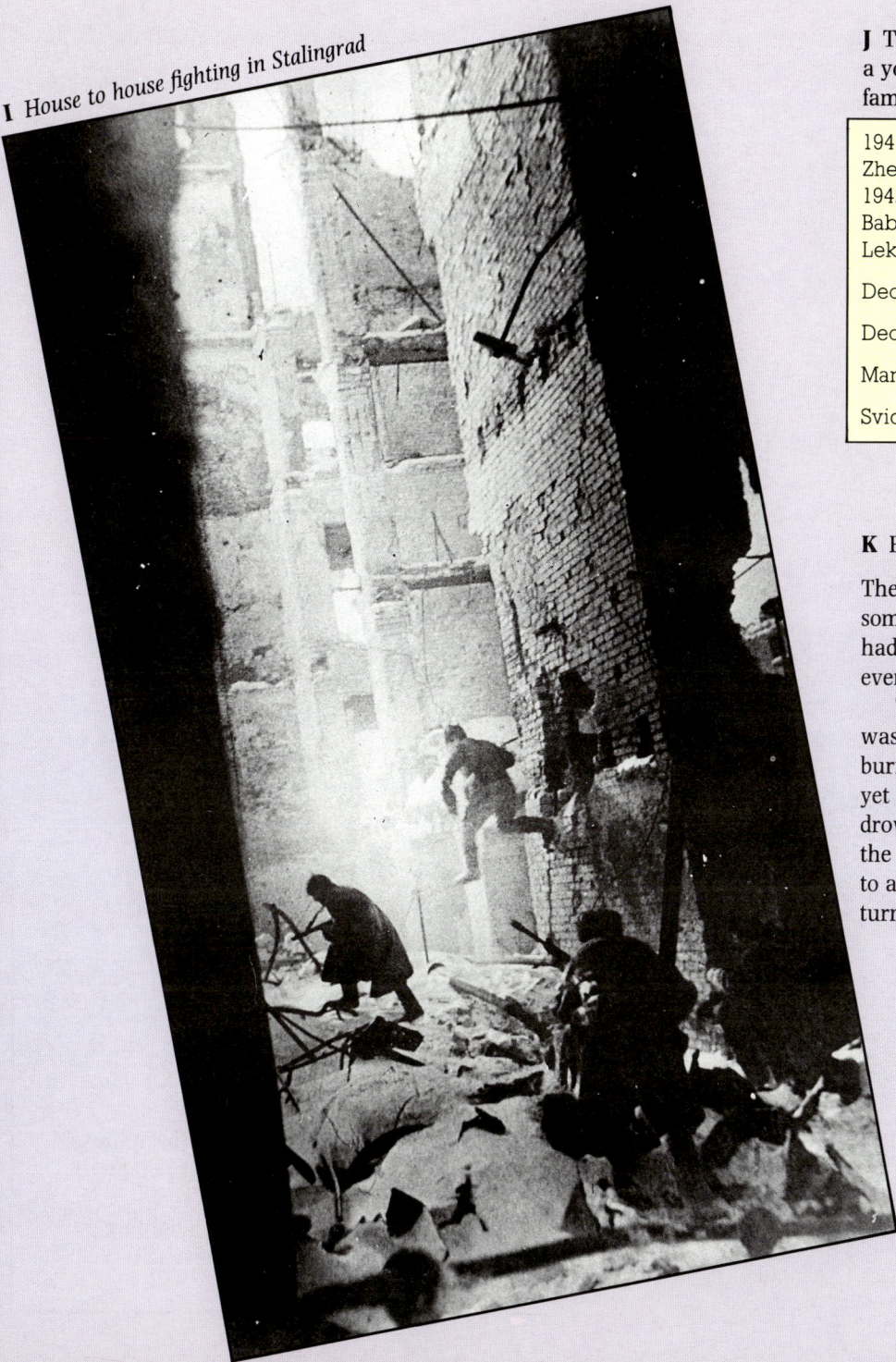

I House to house fighting in Stalingrad

J These entries from the diary of Tanya Savicheva, a young Leningrad girl, tell the tragic story of her family.

1941
Zhenya died on December 28, 12.30 in the morning.
1942
Babushka died on January 25, 3 o'clock.
Leka died on March 17, 5 o'clock in the morning.

Dedya Vasya died on April 13, 2 o'clock at night.

Dedya Lisha on May 10, 4 o'clock in the afternoon.

Mama died on May 13, 7.30 am.

Svichevs died. All died. Only Tanya remains.

K From *Total War* by Calvocoressi and Wint, 1972.

The city (Stalingrad) had been turned into something which none of those who fought there had ever imagined and none who survived could ever forget.

The closest and the bloodiest battle of the War was fought among the stumps of buildings burnt or burning. From afar Stalingrad looked like a furnace, yet inside men froze. Dogs rushed into the Volga to drown rather than endure any longer the perils of the shore. The no less desperate men were reduced to automatons obeying orders until it came to their turn to die, human only in their suffering.

L A German lieutenant of the Panzer Division wrote:

And imagine Stalingrad: 80 days and 80 nights of hand-to-hand struggles. The street is no longer measured by metres but by corpses ... Stalingrad is no longer a town ... The hardest stones cannot bear it for long; only men endure.

M A German general remembers the Russian Campaign:

The Russian soldier values his own life no more than those of his comrades. Life is not precious to him. He is immune to the most incredible hardships, and does not even appear to notice them; he seems equally indifferent to bombs and shells.

Those arctic blasts that had taken us by surprise cut through our troops. In a couple of days there were 150 000 casualties from frostbite alone. A couple of days later our winter clothing arrived ... Sixteen greatcoats and sixteen pairs of winter boots to be shared among a battalion of 800 men.

N Rosenberg, Germany Minister of Eastern Territory, wrote to General Keitel:

The fate of the Soviet POWs in Germany is a tragedy of the greatest extent. Of the three million of them a large part have starved or died because of the hazards of the weather. The camp Commanders have forbidden food to the prisoners; they have let them starve to death.

Even on the march to the camps the civilian population was not allowed to give the prisoners food. When the prisoners could no longer keep up with the march because of hunger and exhaustion, they were shot before the eyes of the horrified civilian population and the corpses were left.

O A. Werth, A Sunday Times journalist, 1964:

The ninth of May 1945 was the day of victory, an unforgettable day bringing forth a spontaneous joy ... of a quality and depth I had never seen in Moscow before. People hugged each other, they were so happy they did not even get drunk.

Nothing like this had ever happened in Moscow before. For once Moscow had thrown all reserve and restraint to the wind.

P With the defeat of Germany some Russians felt that Stalin's policy was right. A supporter said:

'The result of the Battle of Stalingrad showed that Stalin's basic line had been correct.'

A critic replied:

'Perhaps if a different policy had been followed the Germans would not have got as far as Stalingrad.'

Q From *Total War* by Calvocoressi and Wint, 1972.

The Russo-German campaigns were the most terrible war that has ever been waged. The numbers of dead were huge.

If the weather was fine men might go through the motions of ordinary life and, with their singing and horseplay, behave as though they were on an excursion rather than a highly organised killing. But then for many months there would be slush and mud and clothes never really dry, or the intense cold which made it dangerous to take off a glove.

The most remarkable thing about this war was that on both sides men went on fighting it for nearly four years.

Questions

1 Explain how the people of Russia might have felt about:
   a) The invasion and occupation of the Ukraine. 4
   b) The sieges of Leningrad and Stalingrad. 4
   c) The living conditions during the war. 4
   d) Victory in the war. 4
2 What do you think might have been the attitudes of the Russian people to Stalin as a war leader? 8
3 How do you think that soldiers fighting on the Eastern Front might have felt about the war? 6

Chapter 12 The build up to the Cold War

A study in causation

Russia was an ally of Britain and America during the Second World War. However the alliance was often tense. When the war was over the alliance came to an end and relations between America and Russia deteriorated into what was called the Cold War. We can see, in this chapter, some of the reasons why relations became so strained and dangerous.

A From *The Second World War* by W. Churchill, 1954. In October 1944 Churchill met Stalin in Moscow. Churchill relates:

I said 'Let us settle our affairs in the Balkans. Your armies are in Rumania and Bulgaria. So far as Britain and Russia are concerned how would it do for you to have 90% predominance (control) in Rumania, for us to have 90% of the say in Greece, and then go 50/50 in Yugoslavia'.

(Churchill then wrote out the percentage figures on a half sheet of paper, adding Hungary 50/50, Bulgaria 75/25 (to Soviet advantage).)

I pushed this across to Stalin ... there was a slight pause. Then he took his blue pencil and made a large tick upon it. At length I said 'Might it not be thought rather cynical if it seemed we had disposed of these issues, so fateful to millions of people, in such an offhand manner? Let us burn the paper'. 'No, you keep it' said Stalin.

B *The Russian take-over of Eastern Europe, 1945–1949*

Legend:
— Iron curtain from 1948
States annexed by Russia in 1945 and those which became Communist between 1945 and 1948

C From *The Cold War* by Hugh Higgins, 1974.

When Churchill returned from his time in Moscow he said that 'Poland should be allowed to model (have) the government in any way her people choose ... provided it is not on fascist lines, and provided that Poland stands loyally as a friend of Russia'. Thus he openly endorsed (accepted) Stalin's policy that only a government friendly to the Soviets would be acceptable in Poland.

D From a conversation between Stalin and Djilas.

Perhaps you think that because we are allies of the English we have forgotten who they are and who Churchill is. They find nothing sweeter than to trick their allies. And Churchill? Churchill is the kind who, if you don't watch him, will slip a kopek out of your pocket ... And Roosevelt? Roosevelt is not like that – he dips his hand only for bigger coins.

E From *The Cold War* by Hugh Higgins, 1974.

The Polish question was the most crucial, especially since the way it was settled helped to determine the fate of the whole of Eastern Europe.

Roosevelt and Churchill agreed that the Lublin Committee [a Communist dominated government] should be the government.

Stalin, in return, guaranteed to include in the government representation of the London Poles [Polish Government in exile since 1939]. He also agreed to hold free elections as soon as possible.

F From *Documents and Debates: Europe Since Hitler* by W. Laquer, 1981.

In Stalin's eyes the Western proposals to establish governments that were friendly to the Soviet Union and yet represented the democrats were a mere trick, a new attempt at Western encirclement. Only Communists were acceptable to him.

G Stalin wrote to Truman in 1946:

Poland borders on the USSR. I cannot say whether genuinely representative government has been established in Greece ... The Soviet Union was not consulted when those governments were formed, nor did it claim the right to interfere in these matters, because it realizes how important Greece is to the security of Great Britain. You evidently don't agree that the Soviet Union is entitled to seek in Poland a government that would be friendly to it.

The Soviet Government cannot agree to the existence in Poland of a government hostile to it. To put it plainly: you want me to remove the interests of the security of the Soviet Union; but I cannot proceed against the interests of my own country.

H Roosevelt died on 12 August 1945. Truman succeeded Roosevelt as President of the United States. From *The Cold War* by Hugh Higgins, 1974.

Truman said he was not afraid of the Russians. Whilst we did not expect to get 100% of what we proposed, we should be able to get 85%.

While the Soviet Foreign Minister was in Washington, Truman began shouting at him in the language of a Missouri mule driver. Truman told him that Stalin must reorganise the Polish Government to include the London Poles and must hold elections.

I From *The Cold War and its Origins* by D. F. Fleming, 1961.

From the eminence of eleven days in power Harry Truman made his decision to lay down the law to an ally which had contributed more in blood and agony to the common cause than we (USA) had – and what about Poland, an area through which the Soviet Union had been invaded three times since 1914 ... the basis of the cold war was laid on the 23 April in the scourging which Truman administered to Molotov, giving notice that in areas of the most crucial concern to Russia, our (USA) wishes must be obeyed.

J From *The Cold War* by Hugh Higgins, 1974.

Blackett said 'The dropping of the Atomic Bomb was not so much the last military act of the Second World War but the first act of the cold diplomatic war with Russia'.

Truman said – about the bomb – 'If it explodes, as I think it will, I'll have the hammer on those boys (the Russians)'.

Byrnes (the U.S. Secretary of State) said 'The bomb might well put us in a position to dictate our own terms'.

This policy was described as wearing this weapon too proudly on our hip. Its effect on the Russians was to increase their suspicion of our purposes and motives.

K From *New Times* of Moscow, 1945.

The Atomic Bomb is a signal for reactionaries (anti-communists) all over the world to agitate (fight) for a new crusade (war) against the Soviet Union.

L From a communication between Stalin and Molotov.

Let them talk, let them think what they wish. This is exactly what I want them to believe … It will come as a real shock to them when we are able to announce and prove the successful explosion of our Atom Bomb … Never again shall it happen in our History that our people are taken by surprise regardless from what direction the attack may come.

O From Churchill's Speech at Fulton, Missouri, 1946.

From Stettin in the Baltic to Trieste on the Adriatic, an Iron Curtain has descended across the continent. Behind that line lie all the capitals of the ancient states of Central and Eastern Europe. Warsaw, Berlin, Prague, Vienna, Budapest, Belgrade, Bucharest and Sofia, all those famous cities and the populations around them lie in the Soviet sphere and are all subject, in one way or another, to a very high and increasing measure of control from Moscow. In other countries, communist parties or fifth columns constitute a growing challenge and peril to Christian Civilisation.

From what I have seen of our Russian friends and allies during the war I am convinced that there is nothing they admire so much as strength, and there is nothing for which they have less respect than for military weakness. If the Western democracies stand together in strict adherence (loyalty) to the principles of the United Nations Charter … if they become divided catastrophe may overwhelm us all.

N *Churchill peeping under the Iron Curtain*

M Churchill's telegram to Truman, May 1945.

I am profoundly concerned about the European situation. The newspapers are full of great movements of American armies out of Europe. Our armies are likely to be reduced.

Meanwhile what is to happen about Russia? I have always worked for friendship of Russia, but like you I feel deep anxiety because of their misinterpretation of the Yalta discussions.

What will be the position in a year or two when the British and American armies have faded and Russia may choose to keep two or three hundred divisions on active service.

P From Stalin's Reply to Churchill's speech, 1946.

Mr Churchill now takes the stand of the warmongers and he is not alone. He has friends not only in Britain, but in the United States.

The following circumstances should not be forgotten. The Germans made their invasion of the USSR through Finland, Poland, Rumania, Bulgaria and Hungary … Governments hostile to the Soviet Union existed in those countries. As a result of the German invasion the Soviet Union has lost irretrievably (beyond repair) in the fighting against the Germans. In other words the Soviet Union's loss of life has been several times greater than that of Britain and the United States put together. And so what can be surprising about the fact that the Soviet Union, anxious for its future safety, is trying to see to it that governments loyal to the Soviet Union should exist in these countries? How can anyone who has not taken leave of his senses describe these peaceful hopes of the Soviet Union as expansionist.

Question

1 The Soviet Union, Britain and the USA were allies at the time of Source **A**, but by the time of Sources **O** and **P** the Cold War had begun. What were the causes of this, the start of the Cold War? (30)

Chapter 13 The early years of the Cold War, 1947–1949

A study in the interpretation and evaluation of evidence

The Cold War was not a war like the Second World War, or the Gulf War (between Iran and Iraq); there were no battles between the superpowers. But they were still deadly enemies. This emnity can be seen in a number of quarrels from 1947 to 1949.

Greece was torn asunder by a civil war between the communists and anti-communists. In 1947 the British Government said that it could not afford to help the anti-communists any longer. Truman wanted America to step in to help the anti-communist forces in Greece. He announced his intention in a speech that has become known as the Truman Doctrine.

A From 'The Truman Doctrine', 1947.

I believe it must be the policy of the United States to support free peoples who are resisting attempted subjugation (control) by armed minorities or by outside pressure. I believe that we must assist free peoples to work out their own destinies in their own way. I believe that our help should be primarily through economic and financial aid.

C In 1947 the American Secretary of State, George Marshall, announced his plan to give billions of dollars in aid to Europe. This has become known as the Marshall Plan, or Marshall Aid. This is an extract from a speech by Marshall introducing the Marshall Plan.

The United States should do whatever it is able to do to assist in the return of normal economic health in the world, without which there can be no political stability and no assured peace. Our policy is directed not against any country or doctrine, but against hunger, poverty, desperation and chaos. Its purpose should be the revival of a working economy in the world so as to permit the emergence of political and social conditions in which free institutions can exist.

B A Russian historian's view of the Truman Doctrine, 1948.

The next step along the road of worsening relations with the USSR was the Truman Doctrine, which meant in reality the re-armament of Greece and Turkey and building bases in these countries for American stategic bombers. These actions were screened, of course, by pompous pronouncements about defending democracy and peace.

D *The Marshall Plan propping up Europe and saving the US*

E A Russian historian's view, written in 1948, of the Marshall Plan.

Thus the Marshall Plan, widely advertised as a plan to 'save peace' was essentially aimed at uniting bourgeois countries on an anti-Soviet basis. Even right wing politicians and publicists (supporters in the press) saw the Marshall Plan as the nucleus (beginning) of a new Holy Alliance against communism.

F Truman wrote in 1948.

The Marshall Plan will go down in history as one of America's greatest contributions to the peace of the world. I think that the world now realises that without the Marshall Plan it would have been difficult for Western Europe to remain free from the tyranny of communism. Russia was caught off guard by the Marshall Plan. Moscow soon realised that when the Marshall Plan began to function the opportunity to communize Western Europe would be lost.

G From an article in *Pioners Kayen Pravda* (a communist youth newspaper).

President Truman has announced the following principles of American Foreign Policy: The United States will everywhere support, with weapons and money, reactionaries, fascists who are hateful to their own people but who, on the other hand, are ready to place their country under American control. Two countries suitable for this were found at once: Greece and Turkey. Now they both have in fact come under American domination.

Americans are building their military bases there, American capitalists are opening businesses and buying up all that seems to them profitable. For this the Greek and Turkish reactionaries who are in power are receiving from the Americans money and weapons for the struggle against their own people. But Greece and Turkey are too small, and American appetites are great. American expansionists are dreaming of all Europe, or at least Western Europe.

Directly to propose that the European countries become American colonies such as Greece and Turkey is somewhat inconvenient. And so the Marshall Plan emerges in America. It was announced that the United States wanted to 'help' the European countries to reconstruct their war-destroyed economies. Many believed this. But it was soon evident that the Marshall Plan was simply a cunning way of subjecting all Europe to American Capital.

H *After the Second World War Germany was occupied by Britain, France and America (in the West) and Russia (in the East). Berlin was divided in the same way*

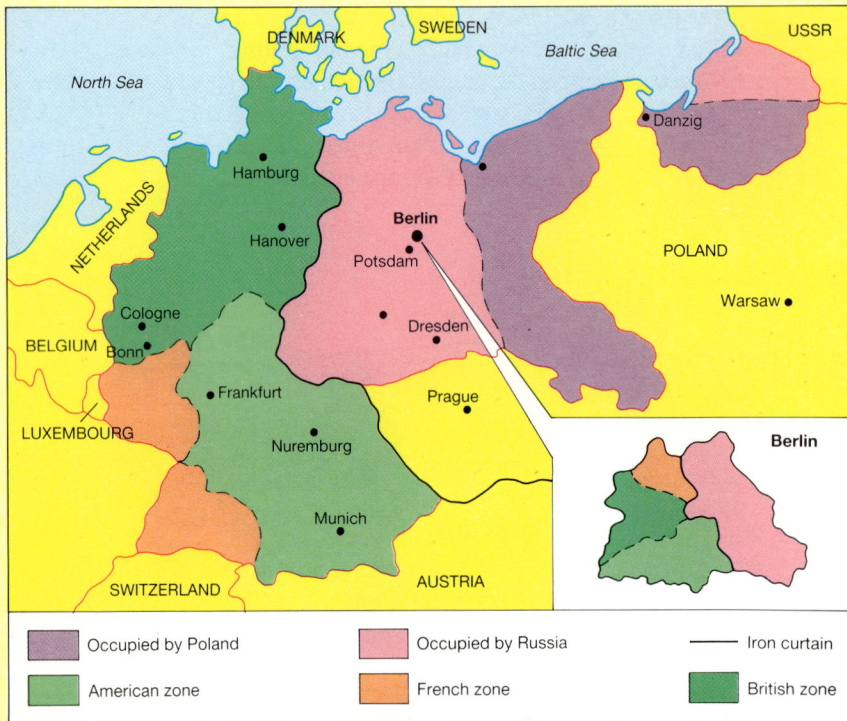

Map legend:
- Occupied by Poland
- Occupied by Russia
- Iron curtain
- American zone
- French zone
- British zone

I *Map of the occupying powers in Berlin showing air, road and rail routes into Berlin*

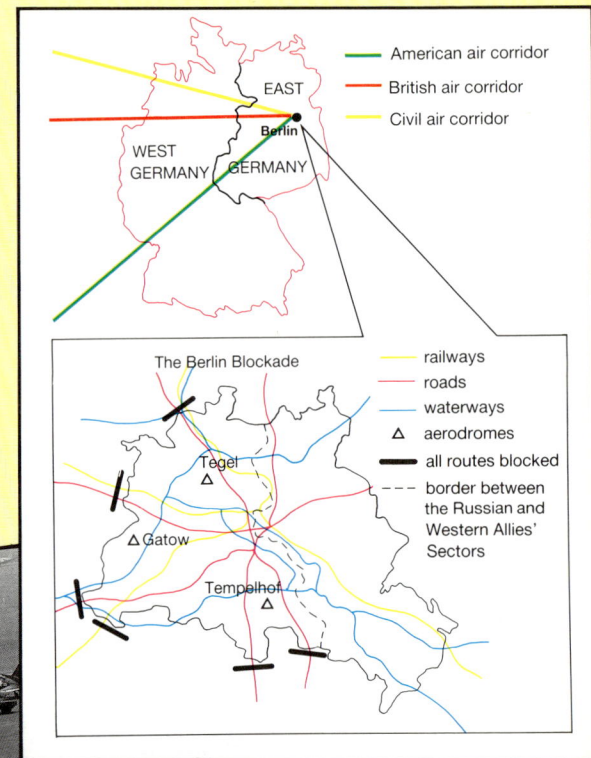

- American air corridor
- British air corridor
- Civil air corridor

The Berlin Blockade
- railways
- roads
- waterways
- aerodromes
- all routes blocked
- border between the Russian and Western Allies' Sectors

J *Relations between the West and Russia got worse in 1948. Russia cut off the West's road and rail routes to Berlin. For ten months Britain and America supplied the people of West Berlin by air. This photograph shows supply planes landing in Berlin*

K *Coal being offloaded after being flown into Berlin during the 'blockade'*

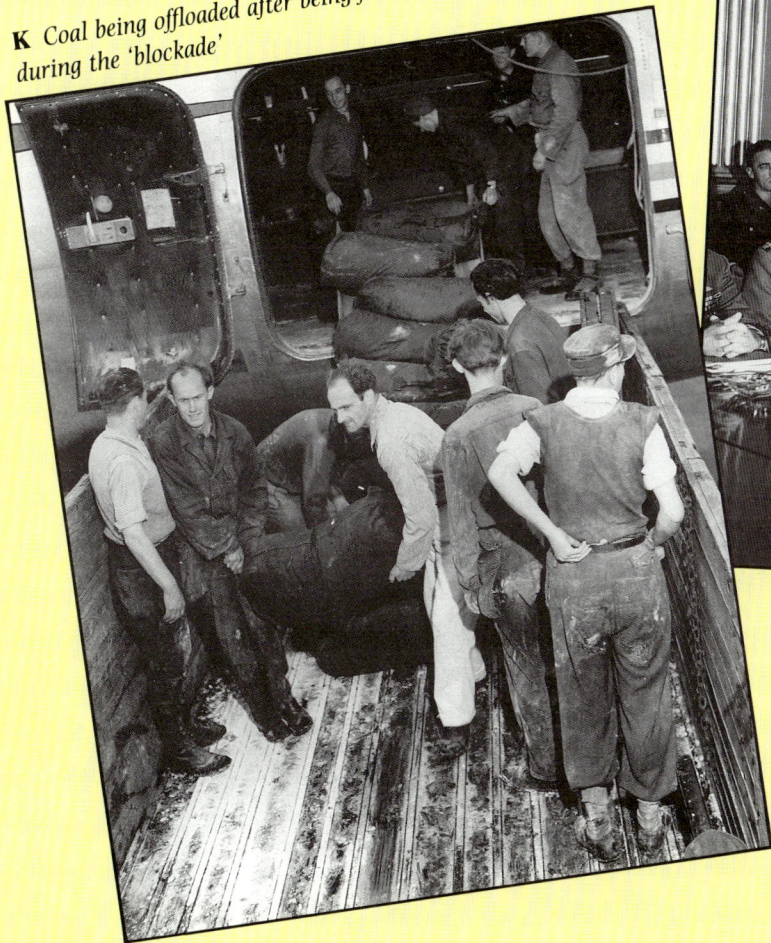

L *The formation of the North Atlantic Treaty Organisation (a military alliance formed in 1949 between the USA and the Western European powers.)*

M *The division of Germany in 1949*

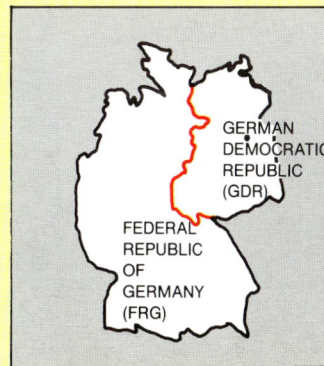

GERMAN DEMOCRATIC REPUBLIC (GDR)

FEDERAL REPUBLIC OF GERMANY (FRG)

— dividing line between FDR and GDR

Questions

1 **a)** What do Sources **A**, **B**, **F** and **G** tell us were the reasons for the Truman Doctrine? 4

  b) What do they tell us of Russia's reaction to the Truman Doctrine? 4

2 Describe and explain the different views of the Marshall Plan expressed in Sources **C**, **D**, **E**, **F** and **G**. 12

3 How do Sources **H** and **I** explain the importance of Berlin to Russia? 3

4 Use Sources **I**, **J** and **K** to explain how the blockade was broken and the difficulties the operation faced. 3

5 What according to Sources **L** and **M** were the consequences of the blockade? 4

Chapter 14 Russian intervention in Eastern Europe

A study in similarity and difference

The Soviet government has kept very tight control over its satellite states in Eastern Europe. Whenever one of them has become too independent, the Soviet government has intervened to regain control. This chapter compares the Soviet government's methods in some cases.

East Berlin, 1953
A From *City on Leave* by Philip Windsor, 1953.

A few building workers on one site downed tools refusing to work to the new norms (increased results demanded by the government) ... A banner suddenly appeared demanding the abolition of the norms. With this the group began to march down the Stalinallee ... joined on the way by the workers at all other sites ... It turned into a march on the government ... They decided on a general strike for the next day. ... About 100 000 marched through the streets ... A number attempted to storm the Economics ministry but were repulsed (driven back) by the rubber truncheons of the police. The rest turned towards the Potsdamerplatz and it was here that the police opened fire. Twenty Russian tanks began to clear the Lustergarten at the same time; tanks then appeared in all parts of the city ... Tanks also opened fire on groups of young people who tried to stop them by throwing stones into the tracks ... By nightfall the Soviet Army was in complete control.

B *Russian Tanks in East Berlin putting down the uprising in 1953*

Poland, 1956

C From *Russia: A Modern History* by David Warnes, 1956.

The 'Thaw' (the easing of tension between Russia and the West) in Russia created expectations of reform in Poland. Communism had not put down deep roots in Poland. Polish agriculture had not been collectivised. The Catholic Church remained very strong, and the deeply patriotic Poles resented the presence of Russian troops on their soil. In June 1956 workers in Poznov went on strike in protest against working conditions. They demanded that Gomulka, who had been expelled from the Communist Party ... be re-admitted to the party and to the government. The strike movement spread rapidly. Khrushchev (the Soviet leader) put Russian troops in and around Poland on the alert, fearing that the Polish Government might lose control of the situation. Then he flew to Warsaw to discuss the crisis with the leaders of the Polish Communist Party. He decided to allow Gomulka to emerge as the new leader of Poland and to purge some of the unpopular Stalinists in the government. Gomulka promised that Poland would remain a loyal member of the Warsaw Pact. Khrushchev calculated that using the Russian army to crush the strike movement would have deepened the Poles hatred of the Russians and would have created more problems than it solved.

D *Khrushchev and Gomulka signing a pact between Russia and Poland*

Hungary, 1956

E *Stalin's statue being pulled down in Budapest (the capital of Hungary) in 1956*

F From *An Hungarian Born Writer* by George Mikas, 1956.

It all began on 23 October 1956 with a demonstration at the statue of a national hero Bena. Fifty thousand people sang the National Anthem, and then fifty thousand people started to cry; students, grown men, officers … they were not ashamed of their tears. A resolution was read out 'We want an Independent National policy. Our relations with all countries and with the USSR should be on the basis of the principle of equality'.

H Here an English journalist remembers waiting for an interview with Nagy (the new Hungarian Prime Minister) in 1956.

In the next room Nagy was arguing with the Soviet Ambassador Andropov. The assistant told me that in half an hours time Nagy intended to declare Hungary a neutral country and ask the United Nations for protection. Russian troops are pouring in from the Ukraine. They are digging in around Budapest. I am very pessimistic. He advised me to leave Budapest at once.

G *The results of the Soviet forces' dealings with opposition in Budapest*

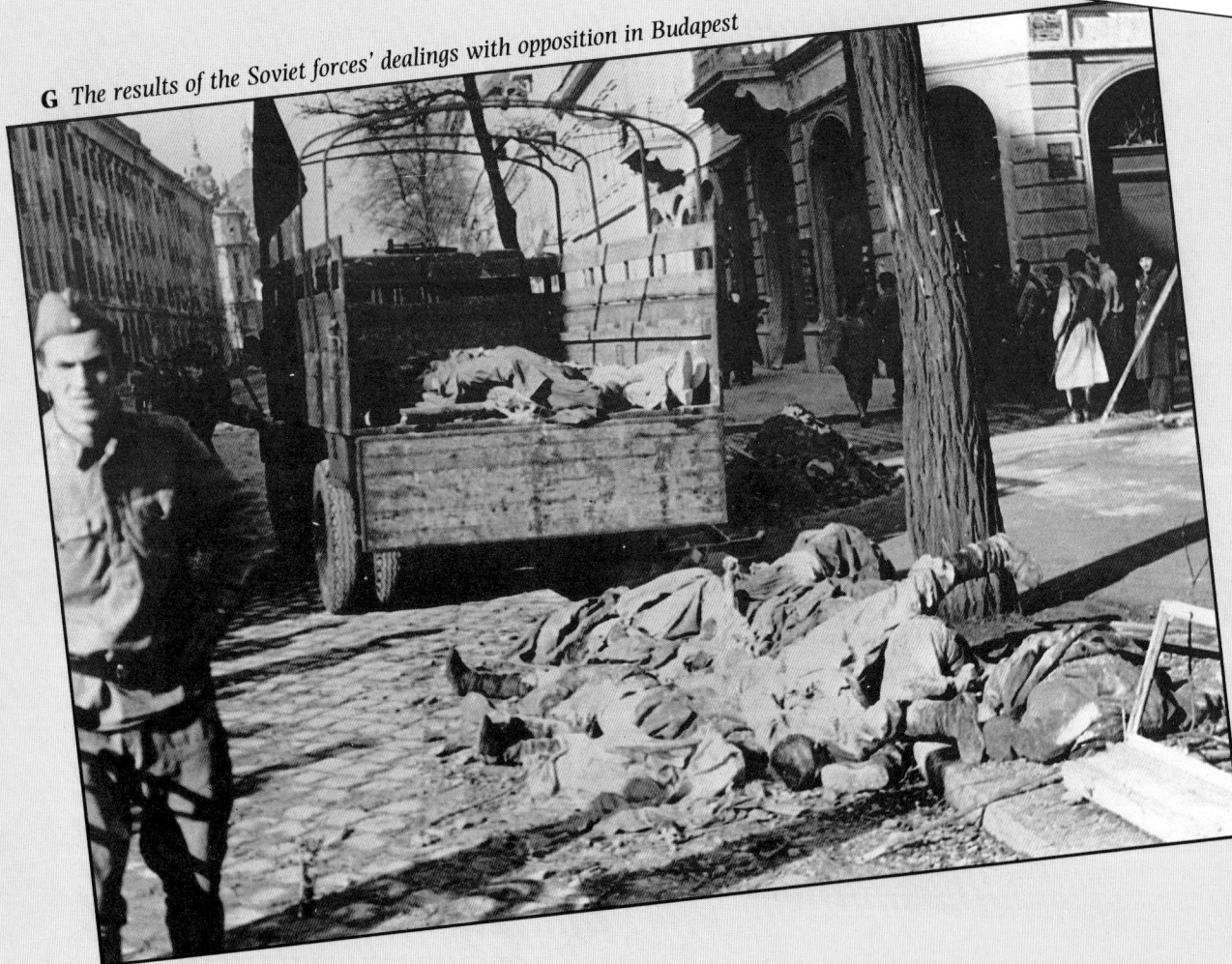

I From *Eastern Europe – 1956–78* by Christopher Donnelly, 1956.

From the Russian point of view the situation had got entirely out of control. It represented a dual threat to Soviet domination of Eastern Europe. The movement had to be nipped in the bud before it could flower.

On the 4th of November the Soviet Army moved into Budapest to impose Soviet military control. Upwards of twenty thousand Hungarians were killed and ten times that number fled to the West. The leaders of the Revolution, including Nagy, were subsequently shot, and a pro-Soviet Government headed by Kadar was established by the Soviet military authorities.

Czechoslovakia, 1968

J From *Eastern Europe 1956–78* by Christopher Donnelly, 1956.

The Czech liberal movement was not a sudden rising as the Hungarian crisis had been. Dubcek, the new party leader wanted to:
1) give Socialism a new face;
2) provide more consumer goods.

These the Soviets could stomach. But the reforms became so popular that the party soon began to loose control.

By July the Czech government intended to:
3) hold free elections;
4) allow opposition parties.

This Moscow could not stomach. Such an example posed a threat to the entire socialist structure of Europe.

Between the 22 and 25 August 500 000 Warsaw Pact troops invaded and occupied Czechoslovakia. Dubček was deposed and a loyal party man was appointed. He accepted that the Kremlin had the whip hand and agreed to form a government to work under strict Soviet supervision.

K *Soviet tanks in Prague in 1968*

Poland, 1980

L *Russia: A Modern History* by David Warnes, 1984

Strikes broke out in Poland over price increases in 1980. The workers demanded not only higher pay but the right to form independent trade unions. The government allowed this and also relaxed censorship and permitted the broadcasting of religious services. The independent trade union Solidarity was set up with Lech Walesa as its chairman. By 1981 Solidarity demanded free elections and the right of opposition parties to exist.

The Russians viewed these developments in Poland with alarm. Brezhnev (the Soviet leader) seems to have calculated that an invasion would result in massive bloodshed, and create more problems than it would solve. He left it to General Jaruzelski (the Polish leader) to deal with the crisis. In December 1981 Jaruzelski imposed Martial Law in Poland and arrested Walesa and other Solidarity leaders. Walesa was released a year later and Martial Law was ended in 1983.

Questions

1 In what ways are the demands made by the protesting peoples and governments of Eastern Europe the same; and in what ways do they differ?   10
2 What similarities and differences can you see in the methods used by the protesting groups to bring about change?   10
3 What similarities and differences can you see in Soviet policy in response to these demands and disturbances in Eastern Europe?   10

Chapter 15 Glasnost and Perestroika

A study of the role of the individual in history

This chapter looks at the most recent revolution in Russia, the Gorbachev Revolution. His policy can be summed up in two words: Glasnost and Perestroika. Glasnost means more freedom of expression, and Perestroika means to remodel or restructure the economy.

A From *The Sunday Times*, 27 December 1987.

PROFILE

Man of the Year Gorbachev

At the end of the last twelve months the Soviet Union is a different place, thanks to him. And in the world beyond Russia, he has been the prime instigator of change.

His initiative has led to the first arms treaty to reduce nuclear stockpiles.

But much more important, is the change in attitude towards his country, that Gorbachev has brought in the minds of the people of the West. Who would have imagined a year ago that a book written by a Kremlin leader would be a best seller in the Capitalist world?

At home the changes are even more remarkable. Compared with just one year ago Russians can now think more freely almost without fear of reprisal. They can emigrate in increasing though still small-numbers. Seeing and reading certain plays, films and novels once banned is no longer dangerous.

However some foreign radio stations are still jammed. There is no prospect as yet of Solzhenitsyn (a writer critical of the Soviet government) being published. Despite the release of about two hundred and seventy five political prisoners many others still remain in the Gulag.

The KGB puts spanners in the works. Gorbachev is directly responsible for the policy of releasing dissidents from prison and for the new tolerance of demonstrations. But the lower ranks of the KGB have frequently caused trouble at otherwise peaceful demonstrations.

B *The dissident Josef Begun being allowed to leave Russia*

C From the BBC, Six O'Clock News, December 29 1987. Brian Hanrahan reporting from Moscow:

When Boris Yeltzin, the most radical member of the Politbureau wanted further reforms Gorbachev backed the Conservatives and sacked Yeltzin.

D From *The Times*, 7 October 1987.

In an open letter to Gorbachev a recently released dissident damns Glasnost, calling it 'A revolution in words'. He said there is still no real freedom to criticise. He demanded a monument to the six million Ukrainians killed in Stalins artificial famine of 1933. He asks why there isn't more Glasnost (openness) about the Ukrainian partisan struggle against Soviet power in the 1940s and 50s.

E From *The Independent*, 16 November 1987. Rupert Cornwell reporting:

Mr Gorbachev is a magnetic figure who has caught the imagination of the world ... The world has responded by sending camera crews of correspondents in their hundreds to scrutinise his country, now more open to such inspection than at any any time in its history. Yet however dominant his personality the Soviet Union still has collective leadership. He must get the support of a majority for his views.

Yesterday Gorbachev promised that he would see through his sweeping project of economic and social reforms ... he did not intend any wholesale rewriting of the country's history, above all the years of Stalin. He did accuse Stalin of unforgivable crimes – although he then praised him for his role in defeating Hitler.

F *A present day labour camp*

G *Russian rock group performing in the USSR, July 1987*

H From a Granada TV programme about the changes in Gorbachev's Russia.

If you want to find the real culture of Perestroika (restructuring), to understand the main pastime of young Moscow you have to hear rock music which the state has at last begun to encourage. It is now acceptable.

The problem of all this activity in the Soviet Union is that it is all being authorised from the top, agreed to by the man in the Kremlin, Gorbachev. The whole Perestroika and Glasnost did not spring from below. It took a political decision from the man at the top; if you like 'a liberal Tsar' Gorbachev. The question really is what happens after Gorbachev goes and how long has he got?

I A Russian fashion show

J Slava Vitseef, known as the King of Fashion, states:

We are a young state, and in its seventy years there have been upheavals, these have prevented us from concentrating on fashion. Now we are reaching a wonderful time when people and state alike are interested in aesthetic education. Now an effort is being made to help industry provide quality furniture and clothes to establish an atmosphere of prosperity.

K Granada TV conducted interviews with people in the street. They asked 'Is Perestroika just another slogan?':

A young woman replied: 'I read the newspapers, if they achieve what they say it will be very good.'
'You don't fear that Perestroika is just another slogan?'
'Some people fear that, but if they achieve only a bit of what is planned it would be a good deal.'
An early-middle aged man said: 'I think it is for always. It is not just a campaign but forever.'
'What makes you think that?'
'Not only I think that, many do: the vast mass of the Soviet people.'
A middle aged man was asked: 'Have you heard of Perestroika?'.
'Yes'.
'What do you think of it?'
'Rubbish'
'Why?'
'So many Perestroikas – Brezhnev Perestroikas, Stalin Perestroikas. They can't Perestroika us'.
'Will anything change?'
'I don't know, we'll see.'

L *Gorbachev and President Reagan after signing the INF Treaty which reduced the number of nuclear weapons held by the USSR and the USA*

Questions

1 What according to the sources are the difficulties in bringing about change in Russia? 10

2 Refer to all the sources. To what extent has Mikhael Gorbachev reformed the USSR? 20